lonely planet

THE
HONEYMOON
HANDBOOK

© LKUNL / GETTY IMAGES

© MURATART / SHUTTERTSOCK

PLANNING ✈

CONTENTS

Budget breakdown

$$ = LESS THAN US$4500
$$$ = US$4500-6500
$$$$ = MORE THAN US$6500

INSPIRATION

© MARK READ / LONELY PLANET

LGBT-friendliness indicator

LONELY PLANET WRITERS HAVE RATED DESTINATIONS FROM 1 TO 5 BASED ON THEIR FRIENDLINESS TOWARDS SAME-SEX COUPLES. 1 INDICATES THE LEAST LGBT-FRIENDLY PLACES, AND 5 REPRESENTS THE DESTINATIONS THAT ARE MOST WELCOMING.

PLANNING

LONELY PLANET'S HONEYMOON PLANNING GUIDE

Getting hitched is the most socially accepted reason on the planet to ditch work and undertake your longest, most splurge-iest trip ever. But before you dive head first into checking off the items on your travel bucket list, take a few minutes to consider the practical stuff, because the trip of your dreams won't just magically appear by itself.

© JUSTIN FOULKES, LONELY PLANET

ABOVE Before heading for the beach, make sure you have your honeymoon planned to perfection; nobody wants to end up marooned abroad.

In fact, lousy hotels, missed flights, lacklustre meals and inhospitable weather can significantly hamper a happy holiday, essentially flushing your hard-earned money down the toilet. And while we can't read crystal balls or do rain dances, we can assure you that proper planning will undoubtedly put the odds in your favour of enjoying the getaway of your dreams.

TIMING IS EVERYTHING

You've dutifully set aside your collection of vacation days – now it's time to work out how to spend them on your honeymoon. It's important to weigh the time you've allotted for your adventure against your destination of choice, and make sure that your trip is spent travelling, not transiting.

With two or three weeks, you'll have a more generous amount of time to take a crack at a faraway destination and overcome the exhaustion of a long-haul journey and/or jet lag. But a week-long holiday, say, is never well served by spending two full days hoofing it from one continent to another,

only to stop a few days later and repeat the gruelling trek back.

The other major timing consideration has to do with seasonality. Tacking your honeymoon on at the end of your already-set wedding date might preclude travel to certain destinations simply due to the time of year. Large areas of the Caribbean, for example, are prone to hurricanes during the months of September and October. Other destinations have annual monsoons – like Thailand, which has two different curtains of rains that sweep across the kingdom during the latter half of the year.

It's best to educate yourself on the high and low seasons of your preferred honeymooning locales. Prices, of course, increase with a rise in demand during the months with the most favourable climate and during busy periods such as school holidays (when desirable hotels can also become scarce). Low seasons, on the other hand – or better yet, 'shoulder' or 'green' seasons – can be a worthy option if you want to see more bang for your buck at the expense of rolling the dice weather-wise.

THE HONEYMOON HANDBOOK

BENEFITS OF DIY

When choosing a destination for your honeymoon, there's absolutely nothing wrong with sticking to one place, but a protracted vacation – as many honeymoons are – lends itself well to exploring several locales. All-inclusive hotels are going to try to convince you otherwise, and travel agents (even those fancy boutique e-businesses) will try to capitalise on your lack of destination knowledge with tours and templates.

However, a DIY trip is much easier than you might think, and the rewards are exponentially greater than signing up for a cookie-cutter tour. Hands-on planning is a crucial part of understanding a destination, and you'll arrive in the country with a commendable amount of acquired knowledge that will further guide you to sniff out the top experiences that really speak to you.

© LOTTIE DAVIES / LONELY PLANET

RIGHT Texture your honeymoon to achieve the right balance between adventure, say, on the streets of Tokyo, and some recuperation time away from it all.

© MATT MUNRO / LONELY PLANET

LEFT Partying in Rio and cherry-blossom season in Japan could be travel experiences to add to your honeymoon wish list.

© MICHAEL HEFFERNAN / LONELY PLANET

HOW TO BUILD A MULTI-STOP HONEYMOON

As the architect of your own multi-stop trip, you might want to think of your honeymoon as a novel; the action on your vacation should swell and ebb accordingly. Think of the beginning of the trip as the initiation phase – you're adjusting to a new world (maybe getting over jet lag) and want to ease into the action as it gradually builds. The middle section of the honeymoon is where the plot thickens. Your pulse quickens with adventure sports, or late urban nights exploring. Then, with the end of the story in sight, the last section of the holiday is when the jets cool – a denouement of sorts when you once again slow your pace. It's the beach in Bahia after Rio and São Paulo, the Amalfi villa at the end of Tuscany and Rome, or the *ryokan* in Hakone when you're wrapping up Kyoto and Tokyo. You need an airbag at the end of the trip, so you feel revitalised by the holiday, not desperately needing another.

© PETEROTOOLE / GETTY IMAGES

THE HONEYMOON HANDBOOK

PiCKiNG HOTELS

Now, with your storybook itinerary you're going to have to slot in hotels. These should play out in tandem with the pace at each stage of your trip, but you need to slightly trick your future self. Every accommodation option selected should build upon the previous choice. The human mind can't help but judge, and when you arrive at lodging number two you won't be able to ignore the instinct to compare it to your accommodation the night before. So, in order to essentially feel like you're winning at travel, each hotel must get progressively better – or maintain the quality of the previous stay – culminating in your big splurge at the end, which nicely coincides with your itinerary's finale. The last slice of the vacation is the happy ever after – just like you and your spouse after the wedding.

© JONATHAN GREGSON / LONELY PLANET

Honeymoon Planning Timeline

☐ ONE YEAR BEFORE YOUR HONEYMOON
Dream. Think about where you've always wanted to go to celebrate your marriage, and get inspired by guidebooks, magazines and websites.

☐ NiNE MONTHS BEFORE YOUR HONEYMOON
If you're budgeting your holiday in tandem with your wedding, you'll likely know at this point what funds you're hoping to allocate to your trip and can compare your budget against that dream list of destinations.

☐ SiX MONTHS BEFORE YOUR HONEYMOON
Properly slot in your travel dates after calibrating for personal commitments and taking into account the optimal time – as you deem it – for visiting your destination of choice.

LEFT To feel like you're winning at travel, make sure each hotel is better than the last.

☐ FOUR MONTHS BEFORE YOUR HONEYMOON (OR EARLIER!)

Cement the foundations of your plans, scouting airplane tickets, booking must-have items on your checklist (hotels, visa, park permits), and firming up a version – in very broad strokes – of what your itinerary might look like (which days in which destination for multi-stop trips).

☐ TWO MONTHS BEFORE YOUR WEDDING (NOTE WEDDING, AND NOT NECESSARILY HONEYMOON)

If you've decided to ask your guests to help you fund your dream trip, now is the time to create an online registry detailing tangible activities to be undertaken at a gradation of price points to suit your wedding guests' varying budgets.

☐ ONE MONTH BEFORE YOUR HONEYMOON

The internet enables the world to move a million miles a minute, so once you begin the 30-day countdown you can take to your social platforms to snoop for upcoming events and trending bars, and even find friends that might be criss-crossing your itinerary.

THE HONEYMOON HANDBOOK ›

© JORDAN SIEMENS / GETTY IMAGES

© MARK READ / LONELY PLANET

© MATT MUNRO / LONELY PLANET

ABOVE If you want to walk the big walk, dance the night away and still have enough cash to visit that world-class beach, it pays to put a proper financial plan in place.

BUDGETING FOR A HONEYMOON

Setting aside your initial excitement, the honeymoon can often be the last thing on your list when it comes to the wedding budget. If you're hoping to kick-off married life with a travel experience that you'll treasure forever, then it's going to take some financial planning.

$ WORK OUT A REALISTIC BUDGET

Start by agreeing how much you think you can afford to spend. Are you happy to commit to less and work hard at keeping costs down?
Or prepared to blow the budget?

List the top five trips you'd love to take. Then research the following costs:

Getting there and back – flights, transfers, taxis etc.	Relative cost of living – mid-range accommodation, lunch, bottle of water, beer)	Getting around – bus tickets, train fares, internal flights, taxis etc.	Visas, vaccinations, medical insurance – any other associated costs prior to travel

Comparing like-for-like costs is a simple way to narrow down your options. Do any of the destinations on your wish-list work with your initial budget? Do you need to set a more realistic target?

Now think beyond the basics. Weigh up your available budget and the experience you're looking for. If luxury is important to you both, make sure you choose a destination where the finer things in life are going to be affordable. A night in a five-star hotel in Deli might set you back US$150, in Dubai it could easily cost US$15,000.

If you desperately want to experience a particular destination, will it be possible to enjoy it on a shoestring? Being broke in Berlin is all part of the fun. Being skint in Vegas, not so much.

What trips and treats do you want to include? Does the destination require you to do certain things to experience it fully? Would you be happy to visit the Great Barrier Reef without diving, or drive Route 66 without a Cadillac?

Once you've decided on the destination, do a proper costing using a website like Budget Tracker (www.budgettracker.com) or apps such as Trail Wallet for iPhone or TripBudget on Android. Make sure you include all the experiences you want to enjoy. Then work out your total costs.

$ GET SOME PERSPECTIVE

The average engagement lasts 18 months. Including flights, the average honeymoon costs around US$4500 per couple. If you're planning on saving, you'll need to put away US$250 per month from the day you say 'yes' to the moment you say 'I do', to accumulate those funds – more if you want extra luxuries.

$ RAISING FUNDS

To get the best deals it's worth booking flights and accommodation early. If you don't have the available funds it makes sense to choose a credit card that offers travel rewards as you spend. Then agree how much you can both put aside each month to pay off the upfront costs, plus save for the extras.

$ OPEN A SAVINGS ACCOUNT

A separate bank or PayPal account will do, but a high interest savings account will mean your money will earn while you save and limited access will ensure you're not tempted to raid the piggybank. Set up a Direct Debit for the same amount to go in each month, just after pay day, so you don't feel the pain.

$ SET UP A HONEYMOON FUND

Most engaged couples already live together these days, so when it comes to wedding gifts more and more people are rejecting traditional department store registries and are instead asking wedding guests to contribute towards their honeymoon fund.

If you want to use a travel agency to help plan and book your trip, ask your preferred agent if your guests can contribute towards the cost. Whether you're planning a budget backpacking adventure with STA or a super luxurious, tailor-made trip with Black Tomato, you'll find many global travel businesses offer a honeymoon fund. In the States, gifting travel has become so popular that American Airlines, Amtrack and Zip-Car also sell gift vouchers.

If you want more flexibility and don't like the idea of having your funds tied up with one provider, there are a range of independent honeymoon funds that allow you to collect cash gifts from friends all over the world, to spend how and when you like.

As a guide, the average wedding gift is worth £60 in the UK, €76 in Europe, $118 in Australia and $87 in the US. Meaning 50 guests will cover the cost of an average honeymoon.

The following businesses operate globally but are based in different countries so check if currency conversion charges apply.

HONEYFUND (USA)

Pros: You can use the site for free if you request guests give cash or cheques direct.

Download the app to get a free account upgrade.

Cons: Adverts on free registries. One-time upgrade fee applies if you want to customise your page and remove adverts.

OUR WISHING WELL (AUSTRALIA)

Pros: You can collect cash via credit card, bank transfer, PayPal, cheque or Money Order. Flexible fee structure means you can choose to pay 10% commission on each contribution or an upfront fee.

Cons: Guests have to create an account to give a gift. User experience not great, especially on mobile.

ZANKYOU (FRANCE)

Pros: You can create a free wedding website to share other information along with your gift list.

You can place gifts on a map. The fee (2.85% of contribution plus a transaction fee) can be be paid by you or your guests.

Cons: Zankyou hold your funds and you can only transfer three times to your bank for free. For the first transfer they need to match your bank account number and Zankyou account and require a copy of your ID, driver's licence or passport.

PATCHWORK (UK)

Pros: Pinterest-style registry means you can show your honeymoon wishlist as a patchwork of images. No need to sign up to try out the site. Guests can use any credit or debit card to contribute funds. Cash goes direct to your PayPal account to withdraw when you like.

Cons: On top of Patchwork's 3% commission on contributions, PayPal charge a fee for their service.

THE HONEYMOON HANDBOOK

$ POINTS AND REWARDS SCHEMES

If you don't already have an air miles account, ask what travel-related rewards your bank can offer you, switch to a credit card that offers affiliate travel discounts, such as American Express, and sign up to store cards that give you travel points as you spend.

$ PACKING ON A BUDGET

Spend money on the fun stuff such as new swimwear and sunglasses. But don't feel you have to invest in new luggage you'll only use once a year. Honeymoon registry Patchwork, for example, lets people pledge their help as well as cash, so it's worth asking if your guests can lend you a rucksack, mosquito net or torch, or drive you to the airport as a wedding gift. A practical way for people to show their love and save you money.

$ WHILE YOU'RE AWAY

It's your honeymoon, so of course you want it to be special. But before you get sucked into buying an expensive 'honeymoon package' at a posh hotel, be clear about what luxury and romance means to you. Is it a penthouse suite overlooking the city, or do heights make you sick? Do you need petals in the bathtub, pink chocolates and towels folded into swans to welcome you? Or would a secluded terrace, an outdoor shower and some fresh fruit do the trick?

Staying in a boutique hotel, guesthouse or apartment is not only cheaper but often offers a more intimate experience than a luxury hotel. Whichever accommodation you choose, think location. It's not only romantic to be able to walk home from dinner on a warm evening, but it saves the taxi fare too.

$ TRUE ROMANCE

Try to avoid expensive honeymoon traps. A carriage ride pulled by a skinny horse only makes you feel sad and awkward. A single rose is not only embarrassing at the time, but annoying later as it lays limp in the sink and then gets crushed in your suitcase. True romance is about love, not money. It's about coming home with happy memories, not debt and dead roses.

RIGHT Prioritise happy memories that'll last a lifetime over awkward romantic gestures that might not hit the mark.

© MATT MUNRO / LONELY PLANET

© BETSIE VAN DER MEER / GETTY IMAGES

LEFT & ABOVE Don't get sucked into buying matching luggage, and think about what it is you really want out of your honeymoon: if camping is more your thing, why fork out for a luxury hotel?

© WILLIAM SLIDER / GETTY IMAGES

THE ART OF COMPROMISE

Most couples know each other pretty well by the time they get married, so are used to making compromises in their daily lives. But travelling together is different. Out of your comfort zones you discover new things about each other. You might share ideals about everyday life but have very different ideas when it comes to adventure. So what do you do?

BELOW If you're a snow bunny but your partner loves the beach, get creative with stop-over options.

© TOM ROBINSON / LONELY PLANET

COMPROMISE, DON'T SACRIFICE

If you love adrenalin sports while your partner is more head over heels for architecture, don't pre-empt an argument by suggesting a beach holiday that neither of you will truly enjoy. Better you're both honest about what will make you happy, then work together to plan a honeymoon that takes into account both your passions.

TAKE TIME TO LISTEN

Discuss your travel wish lists, taking time to listen to each other's feelings and ambitions. Then remind yourselves that your honeymoon won't be your only chance to see the world: you've got a lifetime to explore together. This trip is just the beginning.

NARROW DOWN YOUR OPTIONS

Write down a list of potential destinations, then review and refine your options. Look at logistical constraints: if you live in Europe and have just a week for your honeymoon, New Zealand won't work. Allow each other a veto: maybe your partner loves skiing but the mere mention of slopes causes you flashbacks and cold sweats. It's all good: New Zealand goes on your bucket list of future trips for when you have more time. And skiing gets marked down as 'a weekend with mates', along with your shopping trip to New York.

BE CREATIVE WITH YOUR SOLUTIONS

If there are a few destinations on your shortlist you'd both like to explore, budget might be the decider. If you can't agree on a continent let alone a country, you'll need to get creative.

Mix and match

If you've got your hearts set on different destinations, take a look at popular flight paths and stop overs. If you want to see the bright lights of Tokyo (p82) and your partner wants to backpack around a tropical island or two, you can do both. Coming from Europe, stopping off in Japan on the way to Bali (or vice versa) can be cheaper than going direct. From North America, you can do Japan and Hawaii as a stop-over duo. And you'll get two honeymoons – and two vastly different experiences – for the price of one.

Find a destination that offers extremes

If you want a North American honeymoon while your partner dreams of Brazil, ask why? If you're looking for an epic road trip and your partner wants to explore lush rainforests, Argentina offers both (p130).

Do what you love

If your travel styles just don't match, think about the things you enjoy doing together at home. A shared love of bikes, wine or music could lead to a cycling honeymoon in the south of France, a vineyard tour of South Africa (p53) or a culture trip to New Orleans.

BE OKAY WITH THE ROLES YOU PLAY

Is one of you a control freak while the other is more *mañana*? Or are you both equally interested in planning your trip? Compromise doesn't necessarily mean equal responsibility, but you do need to be comfortable in your roles. If you insist on organising everything alone, don't complain that it's tough. If you don't want to be involved, don't be disappointed if decisions are made without you.

Take the rough with the smooth

If you want to be pampered in paradise while your partner wants to pitch a tent, indulge each other. Roughing it for a few days will make you appreciate your luxury suite and you'll have saved enough money to splash out on some extra spa treatments.

ENJOY THE JOURNEY

Planning your honeymoon isn't just about agreeing a destination and sorting logistics, it's about beginning your journey into married life. Of course you'll want that journey to be filled with love and laughter. But don't over-romanticise – it might also come with delayed flights, rainy days and tummy bugs. The important thing is to enjoy your journey together. Bumps included.

THE HONEYMOON HANDBOOK

(MiNiMOONS

A honeymoon may be the perfect get-out-of-jail-free card with your boss that lets you take a longer vacation than usual, but sometimes life gets in the way and that epic trip just has to wait. That needn't mean giving up on the idea altogether, though. Consider a 'minimoon' – an abbreviated version of your ultimate getaway. If you're short on time but big on ideas, this could be the trip for you.

ABOVE If you're coming from Europe, Morocco can offer an exotic experience without the long flight.

BELOW The French Riviera and Sicily (bottom): concentrated bursts of romance.

© JANE SWEENEY/GETTY IMAGES

© LOTTIE DAVIES / LONELY PLANET

© AARON GEDDES PHOTOGRAPHY / GETTY IMAGES

LEFT Cartagena can provide beaches and culture in one neat package for American minimooners.

© MATT MUNRO / LONELY PLANET

WHY TAKE A MINIMOON?

There are several reasons why a minimoon might work best for you. Some spouses-to-be plan a short getaway before the wedding. This growing trend in some parts of the world is like a palate cleanser in advance of the big day: you've worked really hard to plan the ceremony and the party, and want to step back and find your Zen before saying 'I do'. The more classic reason for condensing your time away is that it's simply not possible to take a long trip right after the nuptials – perhaps work commitments are biting, or you've already got kids. In cases such as this, a minimoon can become the main event or, for some, the stopgap before a more traditional honeymoon further down the road.

THE HONEYMOON HANDBOOK

Where, how long and how far?

Typically, a minimoon could be anything from a weekend to a week away. When planning your trip, consider following this simple rule: the number of hours you travel should not be greater than the number of days of your trip. So, for a four-day trip, for example, you should ostensibly book a flight no longer than four hours. This equation essentially safeguards against two things: crippling jet lag and spending too much time of your short trip travelling.

Ask yourself the following two questions when deciding what destination will work best for your trip:
• Is my destination of choice different enough from where I live and my everyday life that I'll feel the full effect of travel's magic?
• Is my destination of choice different enough from my 'real' honeymoon down the road (should you be planning one) that it will feel like a special trip in itself?

Accommodation

For some travellers, a minimoon is the only way to climb up to the next price bracket. By shortening a stay, a dream hotel may suddenly come into reach. If there's a super-special resort on your Pinterest board, now's the time to book it!

In general, time is extra valuable on a minimoon so it's best to stick to one accommodation and avoid additional hours wasted on transferring hotels and falling into that awkward post-check-out/pre-check-in vacuum between 11am and 2pm. Travellers wanting two stripes to their minimoon (beach and city, say) should target a destination that offers both, like Cartagena in Colombia or Lisbon in Portugal, rather than moving between two stops on one trip.

Itinerary tips

Like a regular honeymoon, an itinerary for a shorter foray should read like a story. The action should gradually crescendo – you've just left the hectic rhythm of your life behind and need a moment to click into vacation mode. The middle of the trip functions like the meat of the sandwich. Get out there and explore, do everything on your checklist (leaving room for serendipity, of course) and joke about needing a vacation from the vacation. Then, push the breaks as you approach the end of the trip.

The last piece of the itinerary – even if it's just one day – is the happy ending. Does the hotel have a spa? Great – soothe those walking legs in the jacuzzi. Is there an incredible restaurant around the corner? Wonderful – enjoy a long, luxurious dinner. This is the time to remember the trip's raison d'être: celebrating each other. The last slice of the vacation should leave you feeling refreshed and poised to return home to brag to your friends.

© MATT MUNRO / LONELY PLANET

© MATT MUNRO / LONELY PLANET

© MARK REAC / LONELY PLANET

ABOVE If you're planning a minimoon, the key is not to overstretch yourself.

ABOVE AND RIGHT Get out there and explore, but don't forget to leave time for serendipity.

© PORTRA / GETTY IMAGES

THE HONEYMOON HANDBOOK

GETTING MARRIED ABROAD

IS AN OVERSEAS WEDDING RIGHT FOR YOU?

Oh, the romance of it all. With a
destination wedding, you can live your
own particular fairy tale – perhaps a
ceremony on a palm-swayed beach,
in the tower of an ancient castle or in
a sparkling ice chapel. Most whims can
be catered for; you could even have
a scuba ceremony or exchange vows
during a bungee jump.

RIGHT If the thought
of a big family wedding
makes you want to jump
off a pier, it's time to
consider elopement...

© MAFELIPE / GETTY IMAGES

WHY GET MARRIED ABROAD?

Free-flowing romance aside, there are plenty of practical reasons for tying the knot overseas – not least the budget. Though they involve the expense of foreign travel, destination weddings typically cost far less than weddings on home turf. There are often fewer people to cater for and you may feel less temptation to bother with expensive extras. You can find good deals on wedding packages and the destination may simply be cheaper in general. Destination weddings include the honeymoon into the bargain, too.

With an overseas wedding you can also have your own day on your own terms. It can be different from the countless other ceremonies you've been to, and free from wedding 'rules' and meddling family members.

However, it is important to also consider the possible cons before committing. It can be upsetting knowing not all of your friends and family will be there – inevitably some won't be able to travel abroad. (Though this could be a pro too...). Still, you can always have a massive party when you get home. Also, some additional paperwork will be required.

HOW?

You could opt for a destination wedding, bringing as many guests along as you can for a festive feel.

Alternatively, you could elope – just the two of you, doing things your way, sharing a special secret. This will cost a lot less, even if you treat yourself to five-star service. And there's always an option to make an elopement video – a growing trend – so you can share the day with the folks back home, virtually at least. Just be warned: eloping may lack the sense of occasion that comes from celebrating with other people.

WHERE?

The world is your oyster. Popular choices include Fiji, Bali, Italy, Thailand and the Caribbean – such spots are so set up for foreign weddings, organisation is a cinch. Plenty of hotels in these destinations offer special wedding packages. You might opt for somewhere closer to home if you want to check the place out before the big day, though in-destination wedding planners and Skype can remove the need.

WHEN?

You've picked your dream destination – but have you checked the weather? A beach wedding might not be so romantic in hurricane season. That beautiful hair and make-up might come unstuck in high-summer humidity; that strapless dress might be chilly if it's the depths of winter. Flight price fluctuation could be a factor too – making your guests pay to fly out on a bank holiday, for instance, could add a lot to their expense.

ABOVE Planning a beach wedding? Just make sure you've checked It's not monsoon or hurricane season when you want to get hitched!

LEFT Keep on top of the legalities of getting married abroad. Contrary to popular belief, you cannot simply turn up in Vegas and get wed on the spot.

Overseas nuptials: the law

Some countries require you to be resident for a certain period before getting married there. Consider getting legally wed at home and having the blessing abroad.

—

Same-sex marriage is not legal in all countries.

—

Required paperwork varies by destination, but you may need birth certificates, passports, divorce papers (if divorced) and a death certificate (if widowed). You may need English translations of these and a Certificate of No Impediment/Certificate of Single Status.

—

If you plan to change your name, you can't travel on your new name unless you change your passport beforehand.

© JRYKI SALONEN / SJTM / 500PX

★ Snow adds sparkle to far-north honeymoons – choose Lapland or Alaska for aurora and activities
★ Around India and Southeast Asia is largely blissful – think Keralan backwaters, Sri Lanka, west coast Thailand or Maldives
★ Caribbean is hurricane-free, balmy and beautiful. For luxury, try St Lucia; for adventures, Costa Rica
★ High summer in the southern hemisphere: road-trip New Zealand or southern Australia (the north is wet right now); get amorously active in Patagonia; go carnival crazy in Brazil
★ Cape Town is a hot city choice. Some parts of southern Africa are rainy; you'll find cheaper, greener safaris in Botswana or Zambia – just pack an umbrella

HONEYMOON CALENDAR: WHEN TO GO WHERE?

© PETE SEAWARD / LONELY PLANET

★ Europe awakes! Beautiful in Paris, Rome, Andalucia's hills, Tuscany and Turkish coast
★ North America warms too – time for city breaks in Texas and Hawaii
★ India sweats (though good for tiger spotting); Indochina veers towards monsoons – pick Indonesia instead
★ Sub-Saharan Africa's still wet. Mozambique's islands and Morocco are ideal
★ Central America and Caribbean still fine, and cheaper as rains approach – squeeze in Antiguan beaches or Cuban culture
★ Autumn hits the south – good for exploring. Toast the grape harvest in Argentina's Mendoza or Australia's Hunter Valley
★ Japan's cherry trees bloom. China's a delight: clear skies, pleasant climes

JUNE–AUGUST 📅

© MARTIN PUDDY / GETTY IMAGES

★ European hotspots heave – sun seekers should try north Mallorca, Alpine lakes, off-beat Greek isles. Scandinavian days are long and lovely

★ Peak months for Peru – it's dry and warm, but also the chilliest (and busiest) time to do the Inca Trail; try Ecuador and Bolivia too

★ Australia's Top End is dry; Queensland's ideal in so-called 'winter'. New Zealand equals skiing!

★ South Pacific is perfect – try French Polynesia, Fiji or Tonga

★ North America? Time for a national parks road trip. Coast-lovers, consider Cape Cod, northern California or Nova Scotia.

★ Bali is brilliant; Borneo too. Seychelles is breezy but gorgeous

★ African safari season – dry, good sightings; head to the Masai Mara/Serengeti to see the Great Migration

When it comes to planning your honeymoon, timing is everything.

SEPTEMBER–NOVEMBER 📅

© ALEX TREADWAY / GETTY IMAGES

★ Mellowing temperatures and kids back at school mean Europe is lovely – try Barcelona, Sicily, Umbria, the Croatian coast, Cornwall or Provence vineyards

★ Fall colours inflame New England and Québec (Japan too); crowds thin at US sights after Labor Day

★ South African spring – super along the Garden Route; Namibia's wildlife is abundant

★ India and Nepal dry up – skies clear in the Himalaya; explore Rajasthan

★ Asian monsoons peter out in October – head to the Philippines, Vietnam or Laos

★ Cooling days make Oman's coast and Jordan's deserts divine

★ Spring in Rio and Buenos Aires; prime time for wildlife-watching in Brazil's Pantanal

THE HONEYMOON HANDBOOK

THE HONEYMOON QUIZ

Not sure where to start with honeymoon planning?
Take our quiz to reveal the type of trip that's right for you.

1. HOW WOULD YOU DESCRIBE YOUR APPROACH TO LIFE?

a) Full of new challenges: I love setting myself goals to achieve
b) Calm and consistent: I find my routine reassuring
c) Super social: I like meeting new people and seeing friends
d) Spontaneous: I'll try anything once

2. WHAT'S YOUR SPIRIT ANIMAL?

a) An elephant
b) A dolphin
c) A cat
d) A horse

3. WHAT'S YOUR SOCIAL NETWORK OF CHOICE?

a) Facebook: I like to show friends and family what I'm up to
b) Pinterest: I'm always dreaming about my next project
c) Twitter: I need to keep up to date on the latest news and trends
d) Instagram: I love sharing photos of all the amazing things I see

4. WHAT SORT OF CAMERA DO YOU OWN?

a) A GoPro
b) An iPhone
c) A vintage film camera
d) A digital SLR

5. IT'S SATURDAY NIGHT. WHAT ARE YOU DRINKING?

a) Just water. I need to be fresh for my morning run
b) A few cocktails with friends
c) A bottle of red wine with dinner
d) A couple of beers in the garden

6. WHAT ARE YOU READING AT THE MOMENT?

a) I'm listening to an audiobook/podcast on my way to work
b) A novel and a book about mindfulness
c) The news on my phone
d) A travel magazine

7. YOU NEED TO GO TO THE SUPERMARKET. WHAT DO YOU DO?

a) Choose what I want when I get there
b) Go online to get everything delivered
c) Write a list and tick things off as I go around
d) Remember everything I need in my head

8. WHAT'S YOUR IDEA OF A ROMANTIC MOVIE?

a) True Romance
b) Dirty Dancing
c) Amélie
d) Brokeback Mountain

9. WHAT WOULD YOU LIKE YOUR PARTNER TO DO MORE?

a) Plan activities
b) Give me a massage
c) Book theatre tickets
d) Take time to listen to me

10. WHAT'S YOUR FAVOURITE WAY TO SPEND A DAY WITH YOUR PARTNER?

a) A day trip to discover somewhere new
b) A picnic in the park
c) Mooching around town
d) A bike ride through the countryside

11. WHAT LUGGAGE DO YOU USUALLY TAKE WITH YOU ON HOLIDAY?

a) A small, lightweight rucksack that won't slow me down
b) A family-sized suitcase
c) A small carry-on suitcase, so I don't have to check in
d) A large rucksack, with space for first aid kit and mosquito net

12. WHAT'S YOUR IDEAL HOLIDAY WEATHER?

a) I don't mind as long as it doesn't hold me back
b) Hot, hot, hot. Me, mad dogs and Englishmen please
c) Blue skies, fluffy white clouds, cool breeze
d) I love the calm and the storm

13. YOU'VE BOOKED A WEEK ON A BEACH. WHAT ARE YOU MOST LOOKING FORWARD TO?

a) Catching my own lobster
b) A full body massage
c) A chance to read
d) Two palm trees, a hammock and a coconut

14. YOU'RE ON A SHORT BREAK. WHAT'S ON YOUR FEET?

a) Hiking boots
b) Sandals
c) Trainers
d) Nothing

15. WHAT'S YOUR BIGGEST HOLIDAY FEAR?

a) Being bored
b) Finding a spider in the sink
c) Seeing a snake on the path
d) Bumping into people. Everywhere

16. WHAT'S YOUR IDEA OF A CULTURE TRIP?

a) Six hours on the roof of a bus, packed full of people and chickens
b) A good book on the beach
c) A guided tour to see some prehistoric cave paintings
d) Watching gorillas in the wild

17. WHAT'S MOST ROMANTIC?

a) Breakfast on a mountain at sunrise
b) Beers on the beach at sunset
c) Dinner by the light of the moon
d) Falling asleep under the stars

18. WHAT'S YOUR IDEA OF AN ADRENALINE RUSH?

a) Jumping out of a plane at 10,000 feet
b) Watching someone else waterski
c) Standing at the top of the Empire State Building
d) Riding a bike down a steep hill

19. WHAT'S YOUR IDEA OF A ROMANTIC PLACE TO STAY?

a) A tent
b) A beach hut
c) A loft-style apartment
d) A tree house

20. WHAT ARE YOU MOST LIKELY TO BRING BACK FROM YOUR HONEYMOON?

a) A lump of volcanic rock
b) A tan
c) A piece of indigenous art
d) A new talent for imitating bird calls

RESULTS THIS WAY
≫——→

THE HONEYMOON HANDBOOK

RESULTS

MOSTLY AS – EMBARK ON AN ACTION-PACKED ADVENTURE

After the excitement of the wedding day, you're looking for a honeymoon that will let you keep hold of that 'top of the world' feeling. Whether it's climbing the Canadian Rockies (p126), skydiving in New Zealand (p90) or skiing in Switzerland, you want your honeymoon to be adrenaline-fuelled. For you, life and love is an intense experience and you can't think of anything more romantic than the view from a mountain top once you've reached its peak.

MOSTLY BS – ESCAPE TO PARADISE

The beauty of a beach honeymoon is that there really are no demands on you. Whether you're staying in a five-star resort in the Maldives (p78), renting a villa in Mallorca or a beach hut somewhere in Southeast Asia (p66), this honeymoon is a chance to sleep late, snooze in the sun and sneak off for siestas. It's about enjoying life's little pleasures – feeling sand between your toes, the smell of sun cream, the sound of waves gently lapping. Pure. Joy.

MOSTLY CS – TAKE A CULTURE TRIP

To avoid feeling a sense of anticlimax after the wedding, you'll want a honeymoon that keeps you busy, interested and entertained. Whether it's the bright lights of Shanghai, the ancient palaces of Andalucia (p146) or the Inca ruins of Machu Picchu, you'll want to explore a new place, experience an alternative culture and learn about a very different way of life – together.

MOSTLY DS – GET BACK TO NATURE

For you romance is about experiencing the peace, beauty and spontaneous joy of the world around you, so consider a trip such as a tailor-made safari in Tanzania (p36) or a backpacking adventure in Borneo. Wherever your honeymoon takes you, you'll want to be outside to see the sun rise, feel the rain on your skin as you explore hand in hand and hear the crackle of the campfire as you fall asleep under the stars.

© CLAUDIA URIBE / GETTY IMAGES

CHOOSING YOUR PERFECT SAFARI

There has long been an association of romance with the wilds of the African bush, stirred by movies such as Out of Africa and cemented by the vast array of indulgent safari camps custom-made for dreamy nights under the stars. For honeymooners, there is a bewildering number of options depending on what you want to see and how you want to spend your days. Here, we round up five of the best trips on the continent.

ABOVE Africa's Great Migration is a once-in-a-lifetime travel experience.

RIGHT Elephants are just one of the majestic Big Five animals you can see on safari.

BEST FOR BIG FIVE

Serengeti National Park, Tanzania
When most people close their eyes and dream of the African savannah, picture-perfect images of the Serengeti will be floating in their heads – its famous plains punctuated with flat-topped acacia trees, rock kopjes and, of course, members of the Big Five (lion, leopard, elephant, rhino and buffalo). Add stunning accommodation options and the Serengeti is a great pick for a honeymoon.

The park, along with the Masai Mara Reserve in Kenya, is also renowned for the annual Great Migration, when more than a million wildebeest and a few hundred thousand zebra travel thousands of kilometres in search of fresh grass – considered one of the greatest nature events on the planet.

Stay here: Serengeti Bushtops Camp (www.bushtopscamps.com/serengeti)
Best time to go: January-February to see wildebeest calving in southern Serengeti; June-September for overall wildlife viewing, with the Great Migration moving up the western corridor in June-July.
Antimalarial medication needed? Yes

Kruger National Park, South Africa
In terms of wildlife alone, Kruger stands as one of Africa's greatest safari destinations – its diversity, density and sheer numbers of animals is almost unparalleled. While far less exclusive than other parks, it has a vast network of roads that are there for the two of you to explore on your own (incredibly), as well as great-value guided wildlife activities. What the pleasant South African National Parks (SANParks) accommodation lacks in privacy, it makes up for in affordability and availability – it's also a phenomenal option for familymoons. For a honeymoon treat, splash out on a luxury lodge for a night or two at the end of your safari in one of the park's concessions, or in the adjoining Sabi Sand Game Reserve.

Stay here: Olifants Rest Camp (www.sanparks.org/parks/kruger/camps/olifants)
Best time to go: Year-round; best wildlife viewing May-September
Antimalarial medication needed? Yes

© MICHAEL HEFFERNAN / LONELY PLANET

© WESTEND61 / GETTY IMAGES

© ERIC LAFFORGUE / LONELY PLANET

ABOVE FROM LEFT Botswana is the best option for luxury safaris; communing with gorillas in Rwanda is a magical experience; Namibia offers spectacular self-drive terrain.

BEST FOR ADVENTURE

Namibia

Hit the open road, hand in hand, on a self-drive safari in what is arguably the most spectacular landscape in Africa. At times you feel like you have this remarkable country to yourselves, it's simply that empty. And being behind the wheel as you drive through the shadows of towering dunes, down into twisted rocky canyons and among Africa's enigmatic wildlife is somehow both incredibly empowering and humbling at the same time. Climbing a ladder each night onto your 4WD's rooftop tent in the wilds, and looking up to the most spectacular night skies, is a truly spellbinding way to experience African safari.

Stay here: Safari Drive (www.safaridrive.com/destinations/namibia)
Best time to go: April-May or September-October
Antimalarial medication needed? If you plan to stick near to the coast or south of Windhoek, anti-malarials are not usually recommended

BEST FOR LUXURY

Okavango Delta, Botswana
At full flood the vast Okavango Delta spreads itself spectacularly across more than 22,000 sq km, yet there are only several dozen lodges nestled in its midst to allow visitors to take in the wondrous nature and wildlife it contains. It's Africa's most exclusive Big Five safari domain and because the rewards are so high, so are the prices. Unsurprisingly, the safari lodges are therefore astoundingly sumptuous, though they miraculously manage to still feel like they belong in the African bush. The guiding here, which can take place in open-topped 4WDs, boats and traditional *mekoro* (dugout canoes), is top notch.

Stay here: Mombo Camp (www.wilderness-safaris.com/camps/mombo-camp)
Best time to go: June-August is the high water season
Antimalarial medication needed? Malaria is rare, but anti-malarials are usually recommended

BEST FOR GORILLAS AND CHIMPANZEES

Rwanda
Going in search of endangered mountain gorillas isn't what most people would associate with a safari, but tracking them on the mist-covered slopes of Volcanoes National Park is an enthralling wildlife experience like no other. And when you finally set eyes on these incredible creatures, you are in for what may be the most exciting animal encounter of your life – a magical way to kick of married life together. Note that you need a permit to visit the gorillas, which should be booked several months in advance through the RDB Tourism and Conservation Reservation Office.

Add to the experience with a visit to Nyungwe National Park, where it's possible to hike through the thick forests to share time with one of our other nearest relatives, the chimpanzee. In 2017, it will also be possible (for the first time in decades) to see the Big Five in Rwanda, with the rhino being reintroduced into Akagera National Park.

Stay here: Sabyinyo Silverback Lodge (www.governorscamp.com)
Best time to go: December-February and June-September are the driest months and best for gorilla tracking, but chimpanzees are easiest to locate in the wet season
Antimalarial medication needed? Yes

TOP 10 BUDGET HONEYMOONS

© MICHAEL HEFFERNAN / LONELY PLANET

LEFT Marrakesh's Djemaa El-Fna; RIGHT Even budget cruisers can afford Vietnam's scenic Halong Bay.

© MATT MUNRO / LONELY PLANET

1) MOROCCO

Arabian exoticism, fragrant spices – and lovely low prices. Morocco's hard to beat for bargain romance. Marrakesh, Fez and Essaouira offer time-warp medinas chock-full of character and cheap cafes. Eschew your sense of direction to get lost in the maze-like souqs – the shopping possibilities are plentiful, with everything from carpets to babouches to be snapped up. Converted riads (traditional courtyard houses) offer accommodation with oodles of atmosphere; some are pricey but many are astonishingly reasonable, enabling palace-like stays on a pauper's budget.

2) INDIA

Long-favoured by the impecunious, India *has* become more expensive – but, mostly, it's still amazingly cheap. For instance, opulent Palace On Wheels trains might be dear, but even budget 'mooners can afford first-class on India Rail – a Delhi-Udaipur overnighter costs around US$20 second-class, and only US$10 more in first-class sleeper.

© JAGDISH AGARWAL / GETTY IMAGES

ABOVE Riding the rails – with wads of rupees in your wallet – in Rajasthan, India.

3) VIETNAM

You could get by for less than US$10 a day in Vietnam and still eat like a king – it's street-food heaven. Make sure to sample the city's signature dishes: beef pho, bun cha (barbecued pork with rice noodles) and chow a bánh mì (baguette) as you wander. A mid-range trip won't break the bank either, but will buy more characterful guesthouses, a better Halong Bay cruise and memorable experiences (a cookery class, a cycle around Hoi An) with change left for a beach stay on beautiful Phu Quoc island.

© BY WILDESTANIMAL / GETTY IMAGES

6) HONDURAS

Honduras is the budget choice in Central America. Inexpensive food and lodgings are easily found. It's also one of the cheapest places to learn to dive. Head for the white sands of Utila to scuba or simply relax by the Caribbean for less; the nearby islands of Cayos Cochinos offer the most romantic escape. Tack on the Mayan ruins of Copán and adventures in Pico Bonito National Park.

© SEAN PAVONE / GETTY IMAGES

5) INDONESIA

Numbers are high, costs are low in Indonesia. Rooms might start from a startling-sounding 350,000 rupiah – but that's only US$25. It's easy to be a millionaire here, so even budget 'mooners can afford plenty of fun. Obvious-choice Bali has great beaches, boutique stays, culture in Ubud, cracking surf. But Indonesia has 17,000 isles! Consider Lombok and the Gili Islands, culture and volcanoes on Java and jungle adventures on Sumatra.

© DANNY IACOB / 500PX

4) PORTUGAL

Portugal is liberating. The little anxieties – is that cafe too posh for us? Can we afford another coffee? – don't exist here. Even in fancier establishments, espressos usually cost less than US$1, beers no more than US$2. You find yourself ordering a second *pastel de nata* (divine Portuguese custard tart) – well, why not? There are cute *casas* and converted farmhouses oozing charm for under US$100 a night, too.

© ROBERT ECKERT / 500PX

7) CAMBODIA

Cambodia is a happy marriage of world-beating sights and budget-friendly prices. It's home to Angkor Wat, for which a seven-day entry ticket costs US$60 – ridiculously expensive compared with everything else in the country; ridiculously cheap for a week's worth of exploring the vastness of the site's Unesco-listed temples and jungle. Cheap beers (US$1), meals (US$2) and ever-improving low-cost accommodation ice the cake.

THE HONEYMOON HANDBOOK

8) BULGARIA

ABOVE Bulgaria offers some of Europe's best-value skiing.

Not the most obvious honeymoon choice, but an inexpensive option whatever the season. Capital Sofia has enough to interest urbanites. Sun-lovers can loll by the Black Sea: soft sand, beers for US$2 – what's not to love? Wintermooners can hit Europe's best-value skiing: Bansko and Borovets have slopes for all levels, plus family-run pensions, hearty taverns and (thanks to that cheap beer) lively après-ski.

ABOVE Spot lions for a song in South Africa's Kruger National Park on a self-drive safari; RIGHT Puerto Rico's capital San Juan

9) SOUTH AFRICA

Safaris aren't usually budget options, but in South Africa you can save by self-driving Kruger National Park's 2WD-friendly roads, staying at rest camps en route. Right across the country, food prices are good and accommodation plentiful, ensuring there's something for all budgets – the winery hotels on the Western Cape are particularly good value compared with those in rival wine regions around the world. The best bargain? The Shosholoza Meyl Sleeper train runs virtually the same scenic route, between Johannesburg and Cape Town, as the luxurious Blue Train but costs a twentieth of the price.

10) PUERTO RICO

The Hispanic islands tend to offer the best value in the paradisiacal-but-pricey Caribbean. Puerto Rico has affordable inns and resorts, plus super sand and more history than most – capital San Juan is one of the Americas' oldest cities. For extra honeymoon magic, kayak at night with glowing plankton in Bioluminescent Bay. For extra savings, go in May: prices are up to 40% cheaper May to early December because of hurricane season (June-November), but in May it hasn't begun yet (p94).

CAN'T AFFORD THE DREAM TRIP? *Try this!*

Try Nepal

CAN'T AFFORD BHUTAN?

If Bhutan's US$250-a-day tourist tariff is too much, opt for Nepal – similarly breathtaking Himalayan mountainscapes and temple culture at a fraction of the price.

Try Croatia

CAN'T AFFORD ITALY?

For lower-cost but still lovely Adriatic Sea-siding, head for Croatia's coast; wine-touring Istria (home to more than 100 wineries) is far cheaper than Tuscany, too (p150).

Try Namibia

CAN'T AFFORD BOTSWANA?

Namibia offers similarly incredible wildlife, but its wildernesses are easier (and cheaper) to explore thanks to good roads, suitable for 2WD self-drive.

Try mainland Ecuador

CAN'T AFFORD THE GALÁPAGOS?

The Galápagos is an expensive add-on – budgetmooners could stick to the mainland, visiting Isla de la Plata (nicknamed the 'Poor Man's Galápagos') for an affordable wildlife taster.

Try the Andamans

CAN'T AFFORD THE MALDIVES?

These India-administered specks in the Bay of Bengal offer a budget archipelago escape, with added bragging rights.

TOP FIVE

OFF-THE-BEATEN-TRACK HONEYMOONS

BELOW That ends-of-the-earth feeling in Raja Ampat's Fam Island group...

© PAUL KENNEDY / GETTY IMAGES

1) RAJA AMPAT, INDONESIA

As far as Southeast Asia goes, this archipelago of 1500 or so islands in West Papua feels like the ends of the earth. It's the domain of determined adventurers but well worth the effort for couples more keen on seductive tropical scenery than five-star sleeps. Pristine coral reefs and incredible aquatic diversity make this a divers' paradise.

2) BALKANS

The Balkans still feels remarkably untouched by tourism in parts. Skip Croatia's crowds: start with waterside relaxation on Montenegro's Bay of Kotor and Lake Skadar; cross into Albania for spectacular hiking in the Accursed Mountains and golden beaches; add Kosovo for Unesco-listed monasteries and Macedonia for wineries and sunsets over Lake Ohrid.

3) TAIWAN

Think of Asian honeymoon hotspots and this liberal outpost of China doesn't get a look-in. Its tiny size belies its immense diversity: here you'll find tropical forests and colonial-era mountain hiking trails, legendary foodie night markets, lively temples and interesting folk traditions – all within an area off China's southeastern coast no bigger than a postage stamp.

© LINKA A ODOM / GETTY IMAGES

4) JORDAN

History buffs have long adored this liberal Middle Eastern country for its staggering roll call of important religious sites and impressive ancient ruins, but honeymoon destination? Nope. And yet what could be more romantic than a candlelit vigil at Petra's Treasury; a sunset soak in a luxury Dead Sea spa; a night at a fireside camp among the dunes of Wadi Rum?

© MARK READ / LONELY PLANET

5) PANAMA

North Americans know about Panama's glorious Caribbean beaches and easy holiday vibes, but elsewhere its honeymoon appeal is little known. Dive into the old-meets-new atmosphere in Panama City and seek out tropical wildlife encounters along the canal. Then retreat to the Highlands' coffee plantations before R&R on the beaches of Bocas del Toro or the San Blás archipelago, ruled by the indigenous Kuna people.

TOP FiVE LUXURY HONEYMOONS

Cote D'Azur, France

For a glamorous honeymoon in a sizzling setting, the swoon-worthy French Riviera is hard to beat. Wander around beautiful villages like Cassis, sip fine wines outside bistros in the old quarters of atmospheric towns such as St Tropez, and dine in incredible Michelin-starred restaurants, while watching the world (and the yachts) go by.

Seychelles

If luxury can be found in nature, it's here on these idyllic Robinson Crusoe-esque islands, with their emerald forests, secret coves, pure white sands and turquoise waters. For utter luxury and total escape, stay on the private North Island in one of eleven secluded villas, each with a private plunge pool.

Sweden

In Sweden, it's all about unique accommodation, award-winning architecture and sustainable luxury. Stay in secret treetop dens with super stylish interiors, sumptuous fur rugs and pure wool blankets to keep you cosy. Experience invisible service and simple but exquisite Nordic cuisine made using the finest local ingredients.

India

India may be better known as a budget destination, but there's nothing more luxurious than living like a maharaja among the hilltop forts and palaces of Rajasthan that are now opulent hotels. Travel to the pink city of Jaipur and experience sensory overload in the bustling bazaars of the old town, then relax on rooftops at night, with candles flickering in the cool breeze.

Shanghai, China

Shanghai has the same super-bling, wow factor of Dubai but is also enriched by its cultural history. Explore vibrant markets, ancient temples and contemporary galleries on foot. Then head to the 87th floor of the Grand Hyatt hotel for cocktails at the futuristic Cloud 9 bar, where you'll feel the buzz of the city – even from this height.

TOP FIVE

WILDLIFE-LOVERS' HONEYMOONS

1) COSTA RICA

The exposure you have to wildlife in Costa Rica feels almost too good to be true, and the sight of a sloth clinging to a branch outside your balcony coupled with a toucan swooping through the rainforest canopy is enough to make any dream honeymoon. Head to Corcovado, Monteverde & Santa Elena, and Tortuguero for the best chance of encounters and tropical eco-lodge oases.

LEFT What you looking at? Madagascar's unique lemurs.

2) BORNEO

There are only two islands in the world where orangutans can be found. Harbouring spectacular biodiversity among fecund jungles, Malaysian Borneo is the easiest part to explore: safari in the undisturbed Danum Valley, then head to Sipadan, one of the world's top dive sites (permit required).

TOP FIVE

FAMILYMOONS

1) RÉUNION

For such a small island, Réunion makes a big impression. Hire a car for a single day and you can drive through lush forests, cloud-covered mountains, visit the live volcano and still be back on the beach by sunset. As a French overseas department, it's super safe and you can expect excellent infrastructure and accommodation with a great mix of creole and French culture and cuisine. A tropical island with croissants. Yay!

LEFT Families will have the ride of their lives in Cuba.

2) MONTANA, USA

There's plenty to entertain kids of all ages in this northwesterly frontier state of ranchlands, mountains and grizzlies. Pretend to be real-life ranchers, ride a chuck wagon and appreciate the epic scenery from way up in a hot-air balloon. To add a little luxury, stay at a traditional ranch such as Paws Up (www.pawsup. com), which offers familymoon packages and an oh-so romantic setting.

3) SERENGETI NATIONAL PARK, TANZANIA

Africa's staggering, fragile ecosystems are manna from heaven for wildlife lovers and the savannahs of the Serengeti are right up there in the hall of fame for spotting the big five: lion, leopard, elephant, rhino and buffalo. For the ultimate encounter, time your trip with the Great Migration when wildebeest and zebra flood the plains, and big cats and crocodiles congregate to hunt them (p36).

4) MADAGASCAR

Intense and otherworldly, Madagascar is an explorer's paradise with a swag bag of unique flora and fauna that make a trip to this huge, challenging island worth the effort: 5% of the world's known animal and plant species can be found only here. The headline attraction is lemurs, but you'll also find paradisiacal beaches, exquisite rum, fine food and a kaleidoscope of deserts, canyons, forests and sacred valleys for blissful honeymooning adventure.

5) YELLOWSTONE NATIONAL PARK, USA

Grizzly bears, chunky bison and packs of wolves roam the 3472-sq-mile geothermal park landscape, which rests atop a slumbering supervolcano in which mud holes bubble and geysers shoot for the skies.

3) NEW ZEALAND

Hiring a campervan is probably the most romantic and stress-free way to explore New Zealand at your own pace – stopping to eat, sleep and play whenever you desire. If you want gorgeous beaches, delightful driving and beautiful views, start in Christchurch on the South Island, stock up on food, games and award-winning local wine, then just go wherever the mood takes you (p90).

4) CUBA

A beautiful, safe and welcoming country to explore as a family. Travel by bus or private taxi to easily hop between historic colonial towns, classic Caribbean beaches and scenic rural backwaters. The best bit has to be Cuba's excellent network of *casas particulares* (homestays), offering comfortable accommodation and simple kid-friendly meals served at a time to suit you. After which, you can make yourselves at home with a mojito or two (p102).

5) SPAIN

If you're looking for a European honeymoon destination with great weather, good food, a family-focused culture and wholesome outdoors fun, Spain is an excellent option. The mountain retreat at Caserío del Mirador (www.caseriodelmirador.com), with its farmyard pets and childcare, stunning pool and spa treatments in the hills near Alicante, is a dream come true for parents with kids under five.

THE HONEYMOON HANDBOOK

TOP 10 HONEYMOON ISLANDS

RIGHT Clifftop villages and perfect golden beaches make Corsica Mediterranean bliss.

© PASCAL POGGI / GETTY IMAGES

1) CORSICA, FRANCE

For... Hikes, hills, haute cuisine, hidden sands
This chunk of France, afloat in the Mediterranean, deserves its monicker: L'île de Beauté. The rumpled, maquis-cloaked interior – where you can easily forget the world – tumbles to perfect golden crescents, some touristy, some seemingly unfound. There's wildness if you want it (the hiking is some of Europe's best), but also fine food and indulgent retreats, not least Domaine de Murtoli (www.murtoli.com) – possibly the continent's most romantic hideaway.

© GUIZIOU FRANCK / GETTY IMAGES

2) QURIMBAS ARCHIPELAGO, MOZAMBIQUE

For... Dhow cruising, culture
Why pick one island when you can have 30? That's about how many specks of wonderful white sand make up this Indian Ocean archipelago. Among them is Ibo, home to the 16th-century Portuguese trading settlement of Ilha de Moçambique – a must-see. After a dose of culture here, sail between the islands – remote Vamizi, luxe Quilalea – stopping off on nameless cayes for lobster barbecues en route.

© CHAD EHLERS / GETTY IMAGES

4) ALGONQUIN ISLAND, CANADA

For... Adventure, seclusion
This tiny speck of pines on Ontario's Kawawaymog Lake can only be reached by canoe, and is ideal for two. There's a cosy cabin with a second-floor deck and outdoor dining table ideally placed for sunset; a floating sauna bobs in the shallows. Other than that, it's you and the wilderness.

© PHOTOGRAPHER NAME / LONELY PLANET

ABOVE Unleash your inner beast on wild Algonquin Island, Canada.

3) HUAHINE, FRENCH POLYNESIA

For... Blissful beaches, ancient sites
Huahine, a 40-minute flight from Tahiti, is Polynesia at its most sublime (and that's quite a feat). Slopes of tropical abundance sink into eye-searingly blue lagoons; there's culture aplenty, including the highest density of *marae* (temples) in the territory; and opportunities abound for snorkelling, horse riding, surfing or doing nothing at all.

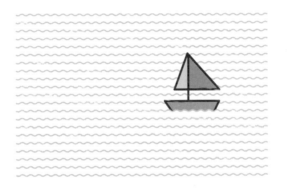

RIGHT Pinney's Beach: a perfect rum-sipping spot on Nevis.

© PETER PHIPP / GETTY IMAGES

5) NEVIS, CARIBBEAN

For... Tranquility, old-school charm
With no all-inclusive resorts or cruise-ship ports, Nevis is as refreshing as one of its gentle trade winds. Accommodation is often historic – old sugar plantations converted into characterful hotels. Diversions include diving, hikes around Nevis Peak and sipping rum on Pinney's Beach.

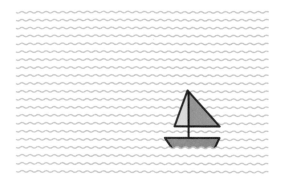

7) PRASLIN & LA DIGUE, SEYCHELLES

For... Paradise, raunchy plants

Beaches don't get much better than the boulder-strewn powdery strands fringing the Seychelles. Ferries run between Mahé, Praslin and La Digue, enabling multi-isle 'moons, and a bit of local interaction. Little La Digue is car-free – explore on foot or by bike. Praslin is home to good restaurants and the Unesco-listed Vallée de Mai nature reserve, where you can stroll beneath coco de mer palms and giggle at their suggestive seeds.

6) TASMANIA, AUSTRALIA

For... Culture, hiking, food & wine

It might not have the weather of tropical Queensland, but Australia's lush southern island state is where you'll find some of the country's best food and wine, epic mountains, cool lakes and hiking terrain. Outside the quaint capital, Hobart, there's MONA – a world-class gallery, brewery, winery and restaurant complex that will simply blow your mind (and where it's now possible to stay in plush, futuristic pods); in the north you've got the otherworldly Bay of Fires, famed for a luxury beach hike that culminates with flair at an award-winning ecolodge.

LEFT With its red rocks and transluscent sea, Tassie's Bay of Fires is classic Australiana.

© JUSTIN FOULKES / LONELY PLANET

© FRANK KRAHMER / GETTY IMAGES

ABOVE Boulder-strewn and beachy, La Digue is a car-free slice of heaven in the Seychelles.

8) SANTORINI, GREECE

For... Unfettered romance, sublime sunsets
Santorini's the sort of spot that might move you to
marriage in the first place: visit this Cyclades isle with a
beau and you're bound to leave engaged. It oozes
romance, with its pretty white houses tumbling down
a part-sunken caldera. Stay in a boutique bolthole
where you can sip Santorini wines on a private terrace
while watching the sun sink into the glittering sea.

RIGHT Quaint
white-and-blue
facades and cool
sunsets ramp up
the romance on
Santorini.

© ARTIE PHOTOGRAPHY / GETTY IMAGES

9) TIOMAN, MALAYSIA

© DIDIER MARTI / GETTY IMAGES

For... Waterfalls, local life, sublime sand
West is best when it comes to beaches in Malaysia, and Pulau Tioman,
56km off the coast of Peninsular Malaysia, in the South China Sea,
has some of the dreamiest. The fine sands and warm, crystal-clear
waters fringe an adventurous interior of waterfall-filled jungle, while
laid-back fishing villages ensure the island retains a local feel.

© JUSTIN FOULKES / LONELY PLANET

10) ST VINCENT & THE GRENADINES

For... All tastes, island-hopping
This Windward Islands group of
32 small isles is ideal for those who
fancy a Caribbean boat experience
but can't afford a private yacht. Public
ferries hop down the Grenadines
Island chain, delivering on-deck local
culture and the opportunity to find
the island that suits you best, from
unspoiled Union to exclusive Canouan.

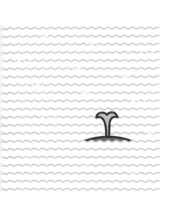

THE HONEYMOON HANDBOOK

TOP FIVE FOODIE HONEYMOONS

Vietnam

Ancient heritage sites, the otherworldly karst pillars of Halong Bay, and white-sand islands have made Vietnam an increasingly popular honeymoon destination, but if visitors come home raving about one thing it's usually the food. Delve into street-food culture in historic Hanoi and take a cooking class to discover regional specialities in Heritage-listed Hoi An. Your taste buds will thank you.

Southern Australia

Australia's southern lands are a dark horse when it comes to gourmet experiences. The world-class restaurants in Melbourne and Sydney play culinary one-upmanship, locals enjoy legendary brunches, and chefs from Perth to Adelaide and Tasmania match top-notch local produce, such as oysters and artisan cheeses, with stellar wines made on their doorsteps (p86).

San Sebastián, Spain

In the northern Basque Country city of San Sebastián, food has been elevated to an art form. Strolling the town's cobbled streets, dipping into bars for pintxos (Basque tapas) and local wine or cider, is the perfect foil for lazy days spent on its city beaches. Add the area's impressive buffet of Michelin-starred restaurants and you're in culinary honeymooning heaven.

Japan

Japan's sushi and sashimi culture is as exquisite as it is bamboozling, but the breadth and quality of cuisine go far beyond raw fish (Japan's cuisine has been awarded World Heritage status). Tokyo has more Michelin-starred restaurants than Paris, and the country's fascinating food culture is in evidence everywhere – from yakitori street stalls to ryokan inns and Tokyo's fine-dining palaces.

Emilia-Romagna, Italy

In a country that lives and breathes food, it is almost sacrilegious to pick just one gourmet hotspot but the holy grail has to be Emilia-Romagna with its *ragù* from Bologna, Parma ham and parmesan from Parma, and its top-class Modena balsamic vinegar. It's easy to explore this region's spectacular gastronomy in restaurants, cooking classes and at the source with local producers.

TOP FIVE

LGBT HONEYMOONS

© GREGORY GERAULT / GETTY IMAGES

BELOW Graffiti celebrates alternative culture in Berlin's Kreuzberg neighbourhood.

© ASK IMAGES / ALAMY

1 BERLIN

A city of bohemian delights and excesses, Berlin is well loved for its alternative music, theatre and arts scenes that quite literally spill out onto the streets – not to mention its out-of-this-world nightlife. For the best LGBT scenes, head west to vibrant Kreuzberg and Schöneberg – where Berlin's Gay Pride Festival is held every June – and east to Prenzlauer Berg and Freidrichshain.

2 ICELAND

Mystical, romantic and adventurous, Iceland is a safe and welcoming honeymoon destination for LGBT couples. Explore mountains, volcanoes and glaciers by foot, husky sled or helicopter. Indulge in some serious pampering at a luxury spa. Then head to Reykjavik to experience the capital's lively gay scene.

3 NEW ZEALAND

Since passing same-sex marriage laws in 2013, New Zealand has actively promoted same-sex marriage tourism to the likes of Australia and other Pacific nations where equality laws are less progressive. Its restaurants and wineries are excellent; its landscapes are breathtaking; and its adventure scene is second to none – the variety of honeymooning options is endless. (p90).

4 CAPE TOWN

This liberal enclave of South Africa is the most welcoming place for LGBT couples wanting to experience African culture, and its creative, outdoorsy spirit makes for a sophisticated honeymoon. Relax on trendy beaches, climb magnetic Table Mountain, then wash it all down with a vineyards tour in the nearby Winelands and a night clubbing around De Waterkant.

5 ARGENTINA

The first country in Latin America to legalise same-sex marriage, Argentina is about as progressive as it gets in this region. Don't miss the vibrant LGBT club scene in the cosmopolitan capital Buenos Aires, and world class dining in the city of Mendoza. If you're feeling adventurous, take a road-trip along the foothills of the Andes, staying at family-run cowboy ranches, award-winning wineries and forest retreats along the way (p130).

© MATT MUNRO / LONELY PLANET

53

TOP FIVE

ROMANTIC ROAD TRIPS

1 AMALFI COAST, ITALY

The spectacular coastal route south of Naples has more than a passing waft of glamour thanks to its reputation as a bolthole for writers, film stars and fashionistas. Starting at Sorrento, the 40km drive to Ravello is a winding clifftop jaunt backed by lush forests. En route you'll pass the pretty towns of Positano and Amalfi, where pastel-hued houses stretch their toes down to the sea.

LEFT Road-tripping doesn't come cooler than on the Amalfi Coast.

2 ICEFIELDS PARKWAY, CANADA

Linking two of Canada's most jaw-dropping national parks through the Rockies in Alberta, the Icefields Parkway is 235km of heart-fluttering mountain vistas between Banff and Jasper. Valleys are splashed with turquoise lakes and waterfalls, and more than 100 glaciers dot the way; hiking trails allow further exploration. Wildlife such as moose and elk roams; pretty Lake Louise has a gondola to whisk you to one of the area's best grizzly viewing spots (p126).

TOP FIVE

INSTAGRAM -WORTHY HONEYMOONS

1 JAPAN

You'll find endless photo opportunities in the incredible beauty of the Japanese countryside. Stop to smell (and snap) the shocking blooms during the *sakura* (cherry blossom) season, head to the Hakone mountains for romantic landscapes, and compose perfect images of temples nestled among Kyoto's manicured gardens and bamboo forests (p82).

LEFT Temples and mountains are perfect Instagram fodder in Japan.

2 MEXICO

Colour lovers rejoice! Fall in love with the hues of Mexico and find artistic inspiration in everything from the brightly-painted buildings, to the traditional folk art and national dress. Head to the southern Yucatán Peninsula (p110) to cast your eyes on a thousand and one shades of blue along the Caribbean coast; and no doubt that perfect street food shot can be found along the way.

3) PACIFIC COAST HIGHWAY, USA

This panoramic highway follows the Pacific coastline, its crashing surf and migrating whales, for almost the entire length of America's western edge – but it's the California stretch (Highway 1) that's billed as one of the world's best road trips. Start in San Diego and finish north of San Francisco in the cliffside town of Mendocino (or vice versa) to take in hidden sands, beach towns and rugged Big Sur. Detour inland for world-class wine tourism at Napa and giant redwood forests.

4) SCOTLAND'S NC500

This new driving route loops the North Highlands, giving access to stunning beaches, lochs and mountains. You might spot dolphins, seals and puffins – not to mention castles, a whisky distillery and remote smokehouses.

5) ARGENTINA'S RUTA 40

This epic 5000km highway runs from the northern tip of Argentina right down to its Antarctic extremities in Patagonia, following the backbone of the Andes. The diversity of landscapes is extraordinary, from desert lunarscapes north of Salta to fertile vineyards in Mendoza, via alpine forests in the Lakes District around Bariloche and down to the Perito Moreno Glacier. Follow this road and you have the adventure itinerary of a lifetime (p130).

3) NAMIBIA

Travel through Namibia's epic landscapes, from the Mars-like red dunes and dramatic open flats to the spooky shipwrecks of the skeleton coast. Camp in the desert and get a shot of the kind of sunset you've only seen in nature documentaries (p38).

4) ICELAND

See things you've never seen before: steam exploding out of the ground, dramatic mountains covered in untouched snow, roaring waterfalls, and shaggy ponies running wild. And if you're really lucky, winter honeymooners (December-March) just might get to see the sky lit up with the phenomenon that is the Aurora Borealis. Quick – take a picture.

5) NEW YORK, USA

This city is people-watching heaven. Get stuck in to the eclectic markets, cheers with cocktails on rooftop bars, and take the weight off at a Brooklyn coffee shop, where you'll be served the most Instagram-ready latte you'll ever see. Then head out among the beautiful buildings and shoot from the hip.

THE HONEYMOON HANDBOOK

INSPIRATION

DiAMOND TiP

BOOKING UPMARKET HOTELS
THROUGH A TRAVEL AGENT AVOIDS
PAYING HIGH RACK RATES.
VEHICLE HIRE IS CHEAPER WITH
MAURITIAN COMPANIES.

Practicalities

✈ Sir Seewoosagur Ramgoolam International Airport.

🧳 Bring a decent pair of trail-walking shoes, a lightweight rain jacket (for occasional tropical downpours) and mosquito repellant.

📅 Tropical year-round, with temperatures between 25°C and 33°C (December-April) and 18°C and 24°C (May-November). Avoid January to February: peak cyclone season.

LGBT-friendly ★★★☆☆
(The government has passed laws protecting some LGBT civil rights, but 'sodomy' is illegal and society is still quite conservative; avoid PDAs)

$ $ $ $

- Beach
- Outdoors
- Culture

MAURITIUS

With waters every shade of blue flanked by gorgeous beaches and coral reefs, Mauritius is an aquatic paradise. Add in wild mountains, epic waterfalls and hiking trails, and this tropical isle offers more surprise adventure than you might think.

Often confused with the Maldives, its distant and decidedly flat Indian Ocean neighbour, Mauritius couldn't be more different (blissful beaches and underwater natural treasures aside). Bursting dramatically from the waters east of Madagascar, this island is no coral atoll – jagged peaks of unimaginable shapes rise above tropical forests, sugarcane plantations carpet rolling hills and rivers cascade off 100m cliffs to frothing pools below. Exciting activities away from the beach abound.

Many of the wild expanses, such as Black River Gorges National Park, are criss-crossed with trails for hiking (and a few for mountain biking too) that will take you through verdant, flowering foliage and deposit you at viewpoints that will vanquish what breath you have left. Looking down over Mauritius' coastline and seeing the kaleidoscopic collision of blue hues between the encircling reef and coastline is simply spellbinding. And it's those protected, shallow waters that are perfect for water-based activities, beneath or atop the surface.

Culturally, Mauritius is bursting with diversity, with Indian, African, Chinese and French ancestries at the fore. Taking the chance to embrace this

LEFT The hulk of Le Morne Brabant rises like a gigantic prehistoric megalith: hike it if you dare.

© MARK READ / LONELY PLANET

© MARK READ / LONELY PLANET

Itinerary

Start in Point d'Esny to enjoy Paradise Beach, one of the island's most beautiful beaches, explore Blue Bay Marine Park (Mauritius' best snorkelling site) and visit Île aux Aigrettes, an island nature reserve with ancient forests and rare wildlife.

≫→

Slide along the east and north coast, taking in the lagoon at Île aux Cerfs and the views at Cap Malheureux before turning south to the tourism hotspot town of Grand Baie.

≫→

Spend your last days at the watersports haven of Le Morne Peninsula – surf, kitesurf, windsurf, sail, kayak or stand-up paddleboard.

≫→

Don't leave without hiking Le Morne Brabant and touring the hills around Chamarel on an electro-bike (electro bikemauritius.com).

ever-peaceful society, by visiting communities or dining on cuisine as colourful and ethnically varied as the population at family-run *table d'hôte*, is one of Mauritius' true honeymoon rewards.

RIGHT Otherworldly mountains add an interesting edge to the blissful beaches of Mauritius.

© OHRIMALEX / GETTY IMAGES

© MUNISAMY ASHVIN / 500PX

KITESURFING

≫→ The coast around Le Morne Peninsula is renowned as one of the top kitesurfing locations on the planet. Experts can use the steady winds to ride the epic swells and breaks outside the reef at 'One Eye' and 'Manawa', while beginners can venture into the perfect classroom – the shallows of the huge 'Kite Lagoon' to the southeast of Le Morne. Yoaneye Kite Centre (www.yoaneye.com), Son of Kite (www.sonofkite.com) and ION Club (www.ionclubmauritius.com) all offer lessons to kitesurfers of every level. The latter also rents equipment to those who already know the tricks of the trade.

Standing like a sentinel, the hulking behemoth of Le Morne Brabant mountain looms large over Le Morne Peninsula – it's so impressive-looking that it's hard to know whether to face your beach lounger to the stunning sea or towards its vertical slopes. However, the 500m climb up it with a guide from Yanature (www. trekkingmauritius.com) offers views that put all else to shame

—

Marriage is about trust and sharing, yes? So head to Grand Rivière Noire and rent a two-person SeaKart for a tour of Mauritius' mesmerising west coast. Take turns thrilling each other while behind the controls of this exhilarating 100hp jet boat.

DREAM DIGS

★ Set on a private sand-fringed peninsula, **Le Saint Géran** is a romantic resort that manages to exude class and style without feeling too formal. Service is top notch, as is the array of dining options – ask for a private dinner at the Tipi. All rooms have sublime ocean views and there are plenty of watersport options. (www. oneandonlyresorts.com)

★ Resting peacefully beneath the towering cliffs of Le Morne Brabant, **Lux Le Morne** has perhaps the most spectacular setting on the island. Although spread along a large section of golden beach, it has an intimacy that belies its size. (www. luxresorts.com)

Practicalities

💼 Bring neutral-coloured clothing (animals don't like white; mosquitos prefer dark), mosquito repellant, hats, binoculars and sports bras (for women).

✈ Kenneth Kaunda International Airport (Lusaka, Zambia) and Lilongwe International Airport (Malawi).

📅 The best time is from June to September, but all lodges are open from April to November.

LGBT-friendly ★☆☆☆☆
(Like in much of Africa, homosexuality is still illegal in Zambia and Malawi, with up to 14-year jail sentences possible)

$ $ $ $

○ Adventure
○ Outdoors
○ Beach

ZAMBIA & MALAWI

The Serengeti and Zanzibar certainly have their charms, but the most exciting 'bush and beach' combo for honeymooners is in Southern Africa. Blending the thrills of a safari in Zambia with the beaches of Lake Malawi makes for an extraordinary African honeymoon.

© JONATHAN GREGSON / LONELY PLANET

© JONATHAN & ANGELA SCOTT / GETTY IMAGES

© JONATHAN GREGSON / LONELY PLANET

LEFT Animals are at their most active at sunrise: prise yourself off your bed for a dawn safari.

Flanked by the mighty Zambezi River and the impressive Zambezi Escarpment, Lower Zambezi National Park is gorgeous and crawling with iconic African wildlife. What's more, the guides in the region are trained to offer you more than just the traditional wildlife drives – you can slide silently past elephants in a canoe, relax with a G&T in a guided powerboat, hike the escarpment for stunning views or track wildlife on foot.

Having this menu of activity options allows you to customise each day to suit your level of energy (after all, you may still be catching your breath post-wedding). And rest assured, even spending the entire day relaxing at the riverside camps is richly rewarding, with wildlife always in sight on the Zambezi. Do try to wake prior to dawn for safari activities at least once or twice though, as sunrise is a glorious moment in the African bush, with perfect light for

photography and animals at their most active.

Combining an enthralling safari with luxurious beach time is a well-regarded honeymoon favourite, and in this regard Zambia pairs incredibly well with neighbouring Malawi. The 'Lake of Stars' has long proved that some of Africa's most beautiful beaches are not on its coast, but inland, and it's now home to some sumptuous accommodation options.

THE HONEYMOON HANDBOOK

Fly into Lusaka, Zambia's capital, before catching a short internal flight east to one of the airstrips in Lower Zambezi National Park. Spend your days admiring the scenery from your riverside lodge and enjoying the activities: walking safaris, canoe safaris, boat trips, escarpment hikes and wildlife drives.

⟫⟶

Transfer to Lilongwe, Malawi's capital, via Lusaka on two short flights. From there it's a three-hour drive or 40-minute flight (plus 20-minute drive) to your lodge on the shore of Lake Malawi. Chill, snorkel, dive, sail, waterski or kayak. If near the southern end, check out the beaches of Cape Maclear and Unesco-listed Lake Malawi National Park. If further north, Likoma Island is great for culture, beaches and diving.

DIAMOND TIP

AVOID THE URGE TO TRY MULTIPLE SAFARI LODGES – YOU LOSE VALUABLE TIME BETTER SPENT RELAXING AND WILDLIFE WATCHING.

LEFT Yes it's a lake, but the beaches of Lake Malawi can hold their own – you can dive, snorkel, sail, waterski and kayak in these waters; when you've had enough of the watersports, unwind in luxury at Pumulani.

DREAM DIGS

★ Minutes from Lower Zambezi National Park and hovering on the bank of the Zambezi, the **Royal Zambezi Lodge** oozes safari ambience. The sumptuous tents all have river views and the sweeping private deck of the honeymoon suite has its own plunge pool, copper claw-foot tub and day bed. The guiding is top notch. (www.royalzambezilodge.com)

★ Perched above the southern end of Lake Malawi among the trees and rugged outcrops of the Nankumba Peninsula, **Pumulani** has 10 gorgeous villas, each topped with grass roofs. Chill on the white sands or in the infinity pool with its lofty lake views. (www.robinpopesafaris.net/camps/pumulani.php)

Gracefully paddling down the Zambezi in a canoe, past pods of hippos, herds of elephants and flocks of birds, is as enchanting as it is exciting (being at eye level with lions on the bank definitely falls into the latter). Together you can join an expert guide in a single canoe, or take to one yourselves (if experienced) and simply follow the leader.

—

Traditional dhows have long been associated with Africa's Indian Ocean coast, but climbing aboard one for a sunset cruise on the serene waters of Lake Malawi is an exceptionally romantic way to see the sun sink beneath the surface.

PRIVATE DINING

⟫→ Dining by lantern's light on your lodge's deck next to the midnight black waters of the Zambezi is romantic, but it can be trumped by a private starlit meal on one of the river's sandy islets. A quiet word with your lodge manager is usually enough to do the trick. Your unsuspecting partner will think they are heading out for a sunset cruise, that is until the boat rounds a bend in the Zambezi and eyes are laid on the linen-clad table, roaring fire, chef and waiter. Eating beneath the Milky Way, to the sound of wood cracking and African nature, is honeymoon heaven.

DIAMOND TIP

BOTH GILI T AND GILI AIR HAVE
ROTATING NIGHTLY HOTSPOTS,
SO ASK AROUND TO FIND OUT
WHERE THE PARTY'S AT.

Practicalities

🧳 Take a torch. The Gili Islands are vehicle-free zones and most of the sandy tracks around the islands are unlit.

✈ Denpasar International Airport, in the south of Bali.

📅 April to October, to dodge the wet season. If you can, avoid July and August when visitor numbers swell.

LGBT-friendly ★★★☆☆
(Bali and the Gili islands are relatively tolerant pockets of Indonesia, but public displays of affection are frowned upon)

$ $

- Relaxation
- Beach
- Culture

BALi & LOMBOK, iNDONESiA

White-sand perfection and a whole lot of fun awaits you on Indonesia's Gili Islands. Then zip across to Bali, where the magical town of Ubud will cast you under its spell.

Whether you want your own private slice of paradise or to party 'til dawn with fellow travellers, the Gili Islands are the perfect destination. Arcing into the turquoise waters off the coast of Lombok, each of the three isles has a distinct personality. Pick the island that floats your boat, or make like Goldilocks and have a taste of each to discover which is just right for you.

Gili Trawangan provides the action, with a large number of diving schools, quality breaks for surfers and a buzzing nightlife where you'll find everything from chilled-out reggae to trance and techno.

To dial up the romance head to tranquil Gili Meno. With its smattering of huts and hotels it is the least developed island and a great option for newly-weds seeking seclusion. Laidback Gili Air falls somewhere between the two, so may just hit the sweet spot. It also has some of the best beaches and snorkelling in the Gilis.

When you're ready to return to civilisation, head to Ubud – Bali's culture capital, home to a vibrant creative community. Explore ornate, crumbling Hindu temples, browse art galleries, get pampered in a spa and spot cheeky primates in the Sacred Monkey Forest.

LEFT Moss-covered stone carvings adorn the temple gate of Puri Lukisan in Ubud, Bali's culture capital.

© MATT MUNRO / LONELY PLANET

© MATT MUNRO / LONELY PLANET

© IAN TROWER / GETTY IMAGES

BELOW Emerald rice paddy fields are ubiquitous in Bali's lush interior around Ubud.

PUMMELLING AWAY WEDDING STRESS

⟫—→ No trip to Ubud would be complete without indulging in a spot of pampering in one of the town's excellent spas. The streets are lined with a dizzying array of places promising to leave you feeling relaxed and rejuvenated – mostly for very reasonably prices, too. Our pick is the Bali Botanica Day Spa (www.balibotanica.com) which is in a delightfully serene setting out of town. Opt for the Romantic Escape for Two, which includes massage, exfoliation and a Balinese favourite: a shared flower bath. Taksu Spa (www.taksuspa.com) is another good choice. Along with couples massages it offers holistic healing, yoga and a healthy food cafe.

Get your honeymoon off to a swinging start in Gili Trawangan by partying up a storm. Shed the hangover with a spot of snorkelling or diving, then jump on an island-hopping boat to Gili Meno for R&R.

⟫—→

Make it a hat trick by spending some time on Gili Air and get some extra zen in the island's yoga and meditation centre. Top off the day by watching the sun set behind Bali's Mt Agung volcano with a cocktail in hand at Mowies (www.mowiesgiliair.com) in the southwest of the island.

⟫—→

Take a fast boat to Bali then jump in a taxi to Ubud (1.5 hours), where you can spend leisurely days exploring temples and nights enjoying Balinese dance performances.

© PETE SEAWARD / LONELY PLANET

ABOVE Each of the three Gili islands has a different feel but all can offer R&R, gleaming strips of sands and teeming marine life.

DREAM DIGS

★ In one of the Gilis' most remote corners, eco-friendly **Mahamaya** on Gili Meno is the perfect retreat for wannabe Robinson Crusoes who like their creature comforts. Opt for a seafront villa, where you can enjoy your own slice of beach and private outdoor shower. (www.mahamaya.co)

★ **Viceroy Bali** in Ubud is made up of 25 luxury villas, each with their own private pool, and makes the perfect hideaway for honeymooners – you can even get married here. Set among lush green forest, the jewel in the crown of this boutique hotel is a valley top infinity pool, perfect for unwinding after a day exploring the town. (www.viceroybali.com)

Essential Honeymoon Experiences

The waters surrounding the Gilis are teeming with turtles, helped in part by the efforts of the turtle sanctuary on Gili Meno. Get up close to the rich marine life in one of the area's top dive spots, such as Shark Point or Deep Turbo. Experienced divers can also explore a Japanese WW2 wreck. Blue Marlin Dive on Gili T is a reputable dive company. (www.bluemarlindive.com)

—

Hire a driver to explore some of Bali's impressive cultural gems such as the temple Titra Empul, which has a bubbling holy water spring within its complex; Gunung Kawi, a lush valley with rock-hewn shrines; and Goa Gajah, also known as the Elephant Cave.

THE HONEYMOON HANDBOOK

© MATTHEW WILLIAMS-ELLIS / GETTY IMAGES

© MATT MUNRO / LONELY PLANET

© NATAPONG SUPALERTSOPHON / GETTY IMAGES

ABOVE Sunset at the crumbling temples of Bagan is a quintessential Southeast Asian experience – you'll wonder why it wasn't higher on your bucket list.

Practicalities

🧳 For temple visits, bring easily removable slip-on shoes or sandals and a sarong to cover bare knees and/or shoulders.

✈ Yangon Airport

LGBT-friendly ★★☆☆☆

📅 November to February is when it rains the least and most cruises are scheduled.

$ $ $

MYANMAR

The serene beauty of central Myanmar's landscape, scattered with ancient Buddhist temples and rustic villages, provides the backdrop for a luxury cruise down the Ayeyarwady River between the old royal capitals of Mandalay and Bagan.

○ Culture
○ Relaxation
○ Beach

© ANDREW MONTGOMERY / LONELY PLANET

© ANDREW MONTGOMERY / LONELY PLANET

Myanmar (also known as Burma) has been enjoying a honeymoon of its own recently as curious travellers have flocked to see a land largely cut off from the world for decades. What many have found is a deeply spiritual and incredibly scenic country populated by some of Southeast Asia's friendliest people.

A relaxing and comfortable way to explore some of Myanmar's headline sights is to join a cruise on one of the luxurious boats that sail along the country's principal river the Ayeyarwady (Irrawaddy) – a waterway immortalised in Rudyard Kipling's poem *Mandalay*. Sojourns on the river can last anything from three to 11 nights and apart from leisurely sightseeing can also include cultural performances and demonstrations of local crafts on board. Most itineraries start or finish in Mandalay, a largely modern city that was a royal capital for less than 25 years in the 19th century, but the real highlight is Bagan. Here, thousands of pagodas and stupas created during the first Burmese Empire some 900 years ago are scattered across the plains.

Even older is the golden temple Shwedagon Paya in Yangon, the international gateway to the country. This is an evocative city worth spending time in to explore the vibrant streets lined with food vendors, colourful open-air markets and evocative colonial architecture.

DIAMOND TIP

THERE ARE ATMS THAT ACCEPT INTERNATIONAL CARDS IN YANGON, MANDALAY AND BAGAN, BUT THEY CAN'T BE RELIED ON TO WORK, SO MAKE SURE YOU ALSO BRING SUFFICIENT US DOLLARS (WHICH MUST BE BRAND NEW) TO EXCHANGE.

Itinerary

⫸→ **Start in Yangon with a visit to the awe-inspiring Buddhist monument Shwedagon Paya. Spend several days in this dynamic city, where Myanmar's promising future is well underway.**

⫸→ **Fly to Mandalay. Climb Mandalay Hill and watch sunset over the city. Tour the workshops of craftspeople and observe gold leaf being made in the Gold Pounders' District.**

⫸→ **Board your cruise down the Ayeyarwady to Bagan, pausing at a couple of villages and temples along the way. Visit the temples of Bagan including the perfectly proportioned Ananda Pahto. Make a day trip to sacred Mount Popa.**

© MATT MUNRO / LONELY PLANET

LEFT Seek out the fishermen of Inle Lake to witness a unique cultural display in Myanmar.

DREAM DIGS

★ **Sanctuary Ananda** is the newest luxury cruise boat to ply the Ayeyarwady. Unlike its rivals, the Sanctuary Ananda is an intimately proportioned craft with just 21 suites, decorated with sumptuous silks, polished teak and gleaming lacquerware. Beds are clothed in the finest Egyptian cotton sheets, the air-conditioning is at your command and an iPad with wi-fi connectivity is at your disposal (though note, it only works while in Mandalay and Bagan). Best of all, each suite has its own balcony from which to take in the passing scenery. Alternatively enjoy company in the Ananda's Kansi rooftop lounge with a cocktail in hand. (www.sanctuaryretreats.com)

MT POPA

⋙→ Although Myanmar is a predominantly Buddhist country, the older religious belief in *nats* (spirit beings) remains strong among the people. A popular day trip from Bagan is to Mt Popa, the spiritual HQ to Myanmar's *nats*. Perched on a 740m-tall volcanic plug sprouting from the lower flank of Mt Popa is the Buddhist Popa Taung Kalat Temple; the views from the temple's terraces make the climb up 777 steps worth it. Before ascending, pay your respects at the Mother Spirit of Popa Nat Shrine housing effigies of all 37 official *nats* plus a few extra.

The best way to appreciate Bagan is from the basket of a hot-air balloon belonging to Balloons Over Bagan (www.balloonsoverbagan.com). These magical 45-minute rides run from October to March and must be booked in advance. Choose the sunrise flights as the cooler dawn air allows pilots to fly the balloons closer to the temples.

—

Visible from almost anywhere in Yangon, Shwedagon Paya, one of Buddhism's most sacred sites, is a mammoth temple complex rising up to a 325ft *zedi* (stupa), adorned with 27 metric tones of gold leaf and thousands of precious gems. Visit at dawn or dusk to see the temple at its most spectacular.

DIAMOND TIP

THE LONGER YOU STAY, THE CHEAPER IT IS – THERE ARE 50% DISCOUNTS ON PART OF THE DAILY TARIFF FOR STAYS OVER EIGHT NIGHTS; 100% DISCOUNTS FOR STAYS OVER 14 NIGHTS.

BHUTAN

Welcome to heaven in the Himalaya. Hidden away amid the world's highest mountains, Bhutan feels like a simpler yet superior alternate reality where you can find beauty, serenity, spirituality, phallic graffiti – and each other.

Honeymoons are supposed to be once-in-a-lifetime, right? Good. Because exploring Bhutan might take most of your savings: you must travel with an authorised tour operator and there's a minimum daily tariff of US$250 per person. This does include all food, 3-star lodging, guides and transport, but you can increase the cost significantly if you want to stay at the dreamiest places – and, well, it is your honeymoon. However, keep reading: it is totally worth it.

There is nowhere else quite like this Himalayan idyll, where the soaring mountains remain forested and pristine; where Buddhist fortresses loom over unpeopled valleys; where prayer flags flutter from every pass and meadow; where traffic lights don't exist; and where success is measured in Gross National Happiness. What could be more romantic than that?

Well, there is something... You'll find Bhutan unexpectedly risqué. There are phalluses everywhere; painted on walls, hanging from eaves. They are the emblem of revered saint Drukpa Kunley, the Divine Madman, and are thought to ward off evil. They certainly raise a smile.

TOP LEFT Bhutan's Tiger's Nest Monastery. LEFT Explore in style with a stay at Aman Resort's boutique lodges.

© JONATHAN GREGSON / LONELY PLANET

© DYLAN HASKIN / SHUTTERSTOCK

Fly into the Paro Valley, home to Bhutan's mountain-flanked international airport and headline site: cliff-teetering Taktshang Goemba (Tiger's Nest Monastery) – a must-do day hike.

»——→

Time your visit to capital Thimphu with its weekend market, or even a *tsechu* (festival). Then continue east over the Dochula pass – admiring the Himalayan views – to Punakha, home to Bhutan's greatest *dzong* (fortress).

»——→

Further east lie the Phobjikha and Bumthang valleys, for more marvellous mountainscapes and dramatic *dzongs*.

»——→

Fit in a hike – perhaps day walks in Phobjikha, the gentle three-day Bumthang Cultural Trek or the nine-day Jhomolhari, a Himalayan classic.

But, ultimately, Bhutan is brilliant for honeymoons because it feels like Shangri-La. It's a place where the modern world has made little dint, and where you and your beloved can get lost amid the mountains together.

© ROBERTO MOIOLA / GETTY IMAGES

© CAROLINE PANG / GETTY IMAGES

ABOVE Bucolic terraced farmlands in central Bhutan provide a counterpoint to all those Himalayan peaks.

DON'T WORRY, BE HAPPY!

»——→ Bhutan is the happiest honeymoon spot. Official. It is, after all, the only country in the world to judge its success based not on Gross National Product but Gross National Happiness. This phrase was coined in 1972 by then-King Wangchuck; as Bhutan began to open up to the rest of the world, he wanted a way to preserve the distinct Buddhist culture and spirituality of his people. Thus he decided that the mental well-being of his citizens was more important than their financial output or status. A noble, enviable decree. And a good philosophy with which to start a happy marriage.

Topping a hillock amid the rice fields of the Punakha Valley, Chimi Lhakhang is the temple of the Divine Madman. Couples wanting to become parents come here – make a small offering and you'll be blessed by a large wooden penis, said to aid fertility; women then pick one of a number of slips of bamboo, inscribed with a name, which determines what they'll call the future child.

—

Traditional Bhutanese baths can be taken anywhere from fancy hotel spas to simple farmhouses: hot river stones are placed in water, where they split and steam, releasing minerals and easing aches and pains.

DREAM DIGS

★ **Uma by COMO** is a cluster of traditionally styled rooms and villas in the Paro Valley, amid hydrangea, rhododendron and camellia groves. Wood-carved furniture and hand-stitched linens add class and character; views of the forest and mountains are sublime. Special touches for newly-weds include temple blessings and picnics on a peak overlooking Tiger's Nest. (www.comohotels.com/umaparo)

★ **Aman Resorts** has five boutique lodges spread across Bhutan – one each in Paro, Thimphu, Punakha, Gangte and Bumthang. The design is rustic-meets-modern elegance; rooms have bukhari wood-burning stoves and great views. The all-inclusive **Amankora Journey** links all five for an indulgent exploration. (www.aman.com/resorts/amankora)

THE HONEYMOON HANDBOOK

Practicalities

 If you plan to visit Sri Lanka's tea country, pack some warmer layers, as it can get cool at night.

✈ Bandaranaike International Airport in Colombo, Sri Lanka; Ibrahim Nasir International Airport in Malé, Maldives

📅 December to March brings hot, dry weather to both Sri Lanka and the Maldives; August is between monsoons and offers the best value deals in Sri Lanka.

$ $ $

LGBT-friendly ★★☆☆☆
(Homosexuality is technically illegal in both Sri Lanka and the Maldives; avoid public displays of affection)

○ Beach
○ Relaxation
○ Culture

MALDIVES & SRI LANKA

Dazzling white sands, turquoise seas and slick hotels with indulgent spas, the Maldives are well known for offering honeymoon bliss – but tack on a trip to explore nearby Sri Lanka's rich culture and magnificent wildlife and you've got the holiday of a lifetime.

© FRANCO BANFI / GETTY IMAGES

LEFT Warning: yes, the Maldives really is this beautiful, both below and above the water line.

© SAKIS PAPADOPOULOS

© TOBIAS HELBIG / GETTY IMAGES

◆ DIAMOND TIP

MAROONED ON A MALDIVIAN ISLAND YOU WON'T HAVE THE CHOICE OF EATING ELSEWHERE, SO ALL-INCLUSIVE PACKAGES OFFER THE BEST VALUE.

Quite simply some of the most beautiful islands in the world, the Maldives offer utter tranquillity and unrivalled luxury in the most spectacular of settings. Each resort is set on its own tiny island, colourful tropical fish swim in the shallows and a private butler will deliver cool cocktails to the deck of your overwater villa. Nothing is too much trouble and no indulgence too great.

Pristine beaches, extravagant hotels, exceptional service, superb marine life – the Maldives carry all the hallmarks of classic honeymoon fare.

However, even the most blissful setting can have its limits and if you think you'll be left craving some culture once you've had time to unwind then Sri Lanka is just a short hop away. A compact but incredibly diverse island, it is crammed with World Heritage Sites and famous for its wildlife. You'll get ancient cities and crumbling colonial grandeur, elaborate temples and tranquil tea estates, and the chance to track leopards or go whale watching – all on an island smaller than Ireland. Top it off with extremely friendly people and a vibrant culture, as well as excellent value for money and charming heritage hotels, and you've got the perfect foil to the excesses of the Maldives.

Recover from the big day blowout on the pristine sands of a Maldivian island where you can be pampered head to toe.

≫⟶

Fly to Colombo and head for Sri Lanka's Cultural Triangle to explore the ancient royal cities of Anuradhapura and Polonnaruwa, the Dambulla cave temples and the towering Sigiriya rock fortress.

≫⟶

Hop on a scenic train to Nuwara Eliya for tranquil hikes across hillsides blanketed in tea bushes.

≫⟶

Watch exotic birds in Horton Plains National Park, swimming elephants in Gal Oya or track leopards in Yala.

≫⟶

Finish up in the historic fort town of Galle where grand merchant houses and colourful galleries line meandering streets.

© MATT MUNRO / LONELY PLANET

© JAVIER SUÁREZ CABEZA / 500PX

LEFT Sri Lanka's hillsides are carpeted in tea plantations and ready for gentle hiking; equally, the ruins of Polonnaruwa should be on your itinerary.

DREAM DIGS

★ Indulge in barefoot luxury without the eye-watering price tag at **Baros**, where you'll get all the powder soft sands and mesmerising views of your Maldives daydreams. Sophisticated yet full of local character, it offers a blissful spa, overwater villas and fine dining as well as the chance to help with coral conservation. (www.baros.com)

★ Blending the charm and elegance of a 200-year-old colonial villa with quirky, modern style, **Kandy House** is one of Sri Lanka's most atmospheric hotels. The nine rooms are kitted out with four-poster beds and antique furniture while outside an alluring infinity pool overlooks lush paddies close to the historic hill town of Kandy. (www.thekandyhouse.com)

MALDIVIAN SURF SAFARI

➤➤➔ Ride virgin waves at sunrise and epic barrels at sunset on a surf safari across the Maldivian atolls. The islands are exposed to the raw power of the Indian Ocean and offer a great variety of reef breaks. Although the North Malé Atoll can get busy, a few days on a live-aboard surf charter (such as Atoll Travel; www.atolltravel.com) will get you to the central and outer atolls where it's just you and the waves. Boats range in size and facilities but the Maldivian reputation for glamorous living rubs off with fine food, spa treatments and often an on-board dive school.

It's not just the incredible scenery that makes the Maldives so romantic but the sheer indulgence of having a candlelit dinner, all alone, on a secluded sandbank at sunset, a private chef to see to your every need and the only sound the gentle lapping of the sea.

—

In Sri Lanka romance comes in a totally different guise on a magical dawn boat trip through Gal Oya National Park, a remote tract of evergreen forest surrounding the country's largest reservoir. Glide through the glass-like water in silence, watching languid elephants swimming between lush islands and tropical birds swooping overhead.

Practicalities

 You're likely to be taking your shoes on and off a lot (as is the custom) so it helps if you have ones that don't need lacing up.

✈ Narita Airport, 66km east of Tokyo, and Haneda Airport, 15km southwest of the city centre.

📅 April-May for the cherry blossom; October for the autumn foliage

LGBT- friendly ★★★★☆

$ $ $

○ Culture
○ Food & Drink
○ Relaxation

TOKYO & MT FUJI, JAPAN

Experience serenity and frenetic fun in Tokyo, staying at a contemporary ryokan in the sky overlooking the Imperial Palace, then retreat to the country for luxury 'glamping' with a view of Japan's sacred volcano – Mt Fuji.

DIAMOND TIP

ARRANGE AN AUDIENCE WITH A GEISHA OR GET DRESSED UP IN A BEAUTIFUL KIMONO AND HAVE YOUR PHOTO TAKEN (WWW. NIHONBASHI-INFO.JP/ OMOTENASHI)

For a relaxing honeymoon Japan's frenetic, non-stop capital might appear an odd choice. However, it can be surprisingly easy to find pockets of calm and beauty amid this metropolis of 13.35 million. For example, the grounds surrounding the Imperial Palace at Tokyo's heart are rarely busy; and the garden hidden behind the gorgeous Nezu Museum is a serene spot to sip tea.

Once you and your partner have regained inner serenity, Tokyo is also exciting and good fun. This is an opportunity to sample some of the finest preparations and presentations of a cuisine that has been accorded World Heritage status; to be treated like royalty while shopping in a grand department store; and to swoon at the city's glittering nightscape from a cocktail bar high above the flickering neon below. And when it comes to hospitality, the Japanese are practically peerless in their practice – not least in the city's luxurious hotels.

On a clear day it's possible to see Mt Fuji, Japan's highest peak, from Tokyo but to experience the full majesty of this 3,776m volcano make the effort to get closer. For some rest and relaxation, base yourself at Lake Kawaguchi, 100km southwest of Tokyo, where (weather permitting) you'll have stunning close-up views of this Japanese icon, reflected in the still waters.

ABOVE The view of Mt Fuji from Lake Kawaguchi – beautiful, isn't it? Be warned it can sometimes be shrouded in mist; summit hikes are only possible late June to September.

THE HONEYMOON HANDBOOK

WEDDING HALLS & GARDENS

>→ When Japanese marry they often do so in purpose-built wedding halls. Tokyo has a couple of spectacular ones that are open to the public, top of the list being Meguro Gajoen (www.megurogajoen.co.jp) – a complex that includes walls decorated with lacquer, mother-of-pearl inlaid nature scenes and painted wooden carvings in the style of *ukiyo-e* (traditional prints). Also take a turn in the lovely gardens of wedding hall Happōen (www.happo-en.com/english). There's a serene teahouse here where ladies in kimono will serve you, while newly-weds pose for photos in elaborate traditional costumes against a backdrop of bonsai, stone lanterns and an ornamental pond.

Spend at least a couple of days exploring Tokyo. Don't miss atmospheric Asakusa, home to Senso-ji, the city's most important Buddhist temple, and Imado-jinja, a popular shrine for those seeking good luck in love and marriage.

>→

Travel three hours west of Tokyo, via bus and taxi or hire car, to tranquil Lake Kawaguchi at the foot of Mt Fuji. Board the Ensolleille boat for a 20-minute cruise across the lake then ride the Mt Kachi Kachi Rope Way, a cable car that glides up to 1,075 meters, for panoramic views of Japan's most sacred mountain and the lake. Late June to mid-September, you can even hike to Mt Fuji's summit.

© LUCIANO MORTULA / SHUTTERSTOCK

LEFT The bright neon lights of Tokyo.

RIGHT Get back to nature on Hoshinoya Fuji's cloud terrace.

© HOSHINOYA FUJI

© HOSHINOYA FUJI

© MATT MUNRO / LONELY PLANET

ABOVE In Tokyo haute cuisine is taken to a whole other level.

Tokyo has more Michelin-starred restaurants than Paris and it's well worth making the effort to secure a reservation at one, such as Kikunoi (www.kikunoi.jp) in Akasaka. Here you can enjoy exquisitely prepared seasonal dishes that are as beautiful to look at as they are delicious to taste.

—

The Japanese have made retail a fine art and nowhere is that more apparent than in the Nihonbashi branch of Mitsukoshi, the grand dame of Tokyo's department stores. Arrive for its opening at 10am and you'll be greeted by a choreographed display of sales assistants bowing in unison as you walk through the store.

 DREAM DIGS

★ **Aman Tokyo** occupies the top six floors of the 38-storey Ōtemachi Tower and takes inspiration from Japan's traditional ryokan houses, incorporating natural materials – including dark stone walls, blonde wood and white *washi* (rice paper) – into its elegant, minimalist furnishings. The super spacious rooms all have baths with stunning city view – something you also get from the giant onsen-style stone bath in the spa. (www.aman.com/resorts/aman-tokyo)

★ Cocooned by a red pine forest in a national park, **Hoshinoya Fuji** is a luxury resort where you can experience 'glamping' at the foot of Mt Fuji. Forget having to put up a tent – here you sleep on soft beds in minimally decorated, chic concrete cabins each with sweeping views of Lake Kawaguchi and sometimes Mt Fuji from their immense windows and balconies. (www.hoshinoyafuji.com/en)

THE HONEYMOON HANDBOOK

© CATHERINE SUTHERLAND / LONELY PLANET

© TROY WEGMAN / SHUTTERSTOCK

© CATHERINE SUTHERLAND / LONELY PLANET

Practicalities

🧳 The southern sun bites like a shark: you're gonna need a sun hat, no matter what the season.

✈ Darwin Airport, Sydney Airport

LGBT-friendly ★★★★★

📅 The Kimberley is only really accessible May to September; go June to August for lower temperatures and low humidity in Australia's northwest, and mild East Coast days with minimal crowds.

$ $ $ $

ABOVE Sydney's Bondi Beach, the vineyards of Barossa Valley and the magnificent gorges of the Kimberley offer polar extremes of Australian travel experiences.

DIAMOND TIP

AUSTRALIA IS STUPENDOUSLY BIG. FORGET BUSES AND TRAINS: DOMESTIC FLIGHTS ARE THE ONLY WAY TO GET FROM COAST TO COAST.

AUSTRALIA

From the remote northwest to the far-flung east, experience the indulgent best of Australia's fiery-red land: adventure in the outback, sublime wine regions, Sydney's sophisticated beach-city scene and a heaven-sent island jewel adrift in the South Pacific.

○ Adventure
○ Food & Drink
○ Beach

THE HONEYMOON HANDBOOK

© CATHERINE SUTHERLAND / LONELY PLANET

All but cut off from the world during Australia's northern tropical monsoon season, the Kimberley is a vast wilderness area of gorges, rivers and waterfalls that defines this country's spirited wild west. Kick off your honeymoon here in a remote, luxury eco-lodge and you're in for a one-of-a-kind outback experience, with world-class canyon hikes, cowboy moments and off-road adventures.

In South Australia, the wine regions encircling Adelaide are custom-built for naughty weekenders. Just an hour from the city are the shiraz vines of McLaren Vale and the famous Barossa Valley, with the riesling-soaked Clare Valley a further hour north. Hop on a bike and wobble between winery cellar doors before retreating to your luxe B&B.

Sydney is Australia's big smoke – a true 'world city', wrapped around the improbably gorgeous Sydney Harbour. Chug across the water on a ferry, dunk yourself in the waves at Bondi Beach, catch a show (or at least an Instagram shot) at the Sydney Opera House then grab a cocktail at the slinky waterside Opera Bar before a ritzy seafood dinner.

A short flight offshore is World Heritage-listed Lord Howe Island, perhaps Australia's most underrated holiday destination, home to a pin-up marine park that hosts the world's southernmost coral reef: the fact that only 400 visitors are allowed on the island at one time guarantees a unique experience and romantic solitude to round off your trip.

Itinerary

Jet into Kununurra, Western Australia, via Darwin. From here it's a direct transfer to your accommodation at El Questro Station Township (see Dream Digs); the perfect base for going walkabout in the otherworldly Kimberley region.

≫→

Backtrack to Darwin then fly

south to Adelaide, the heart of Australia's world-beating wine industry. Rent a car and roll into the vines.

≫→

Wing into Sydney from Adelaide. You won't need a car here – public transport is excellent, and downtown Sydney is

very walkable. Museums, beaches, wine bars, restaurants, jazz joints – it's all waiting.

≫→

Hop another domestic flight to Lord Howe Island for plush resort accommodation and some seriously beachy R&R.

LEFT Sydney's Opera House: a true icon of this crazy far-flung country.

DREAM DIGS

★ A 400,000-hectare former cattle station, **El Questro Station Township** has all the bells and whistles you wouldn't expect to find in the middle of the Kimberley. It's home to the region's best restaurant and rangers can organise any manner of wilderness activity for you, including heli-tours. The spectrum of accommodation ensures it's affordable for all: at the lower end, that's camping; for honeymoon class, book into the adults-only Homestead. (www.elquestro.com.au)

★ Inside the historic State Theatre in central Sydney, sassy **QT Sydney** is totally OTT. The twelve rooms here feature madcap art-deco stylings, retro games and martini kits, plus there's an on-site spa, barber (!) and a hip bar/grill if you don't feel like stepping out. (www.qtsydney.com.au)

CYCLING THE RIESLING TRAIL

➤➤➤ Winding through the vines in South Australia's compact Clare Valley wine region (best known for its summer-scented riesling), the aptly named Riesling Trail is a 33km cycling trail following an old railway line between Auburn and Barinia. Hire a bike or a tandem (complete with wine rack) and hit the trail, pedalling past dozens of enticing winery cellar doors. The super-scenic route is clearly marked and well maintained, and being a former railway there aren't any steep hills! Repair to your stone B&B cottage afterwards with a bottle or two of the local good stuff. (www.rieslingtrail.com.au)

Essential Honeymoon Experiences

Bondi Beach is Sydney's biggest and best – a deep golden arc with the Pacific Ocean rolling in. Backpackers and models rub shoulders with suits and surfers, shuffling between cafes to the hypnotic rhythm of the waves. A day on the sand here is a quintessential Australian experience.

—

Plenty of people come to Lord Howe Island to snorkel or dive the coral-reef lagoon, sail, kayak, or just laze on the beach. Our advice? Don't miss Mt Gower, considered one of Australia's best day hikes. It's an 875m climb to the summit through lush forest, best tackled on a guided ascent (www.lordhoweislandtours.net). Go to the beach tomorrow...

THE HONEYMOON HANDBOOK

DIAMOND TIP

IF YOU'RE DRIVING, DON'T UNDERESTIMATE TRAVEL TIMES OVER SEEMINGLY SHORT MAP DISTANCES: ROADS HERE CAN BE WIGGLY AND TIGHT!

Practicalities

🧳 Layers of clothes are the key to comfort here, as the weather can change quickly.

✈ Queenstown Airport, Christchurch Airport

📅 June to September to hit the winter ski slopes, or December to February for clear summer skies and sunny days outdoors.

LGBT-friendly ★★★★★

$ $ $

- Outdoors
- Food & Drink
- **Adventure**

SOUTH ISLAND, NEW ZEALAND

New Zealand is crazy good-looking by anyone's measure, the South Island in particular offering up vista after swoon-worthy vista. And in among the boundless photo opportunities you'll find boutique wineries, fab food rooms, high-end accommodation and endless outdoor activities.

Queenstown is where you want to be: a hyperactive ski town in winter and super-scenic outdoors hub in summer. Try bungy jumping if you're brimming with bravado, hit the ski slopes, kayak across super-scenic Milford Sound, tackle the epic Milford Track on a luxury guided hike or take an eye-popping helicopter flight over lofty Aoraki/Mt Cook and the West Coast glaciers.

Feeling less energetic? A wine-tasting tour around the nearby Gibbston Wine Region makes for an indulgent day out, with a classy winery restaurant lunch to boot. After dark, indulge yourself in Queenstown's hip restaurants and aprés-ski bar scene.

Further afield, Christchurch is a city on the rise and the South Island's cultural hub. From here, day trip through the mountains from one side of NZ to the other on the legendary TranzAlpine railway – one of the world's most scenic rail journeys – or explore the volcanically hewn Banks Peninsula and the photogenic town of Akaroa, where French colonists planted *le tricolor* flag in 1840.

© CHAMELEONSEYE / GETTY IMAGES

ABOVE New Zealand's southern vines are crowned by snowy peaks.

THE HONEYMOON HANDBOOK

Itinerary

Wing into Queenstown direct, if you can. Wander the lakeside and unwind in the bars before skiing, mountain biking or touring a winery. Sign up for a luxe guided Milford Track hike through fjord country, with comfy lodges and cooked meals every night (ultimatehikes. co.nz), some Milford Sound kayaking or a scenic flight (glenorchyair.co.nz).

≫→

Drive to Christchurch, a city rebuilding with amazing vigour and ingenuity. Wander the Botanic Gardens, cuddle up on an Avon River boat ride, or day trip to the Banks Peninsula for a croissant or two.

≫→

Take the TranzAlpine railway (kiwirailscenic. co.nz/tranzalpine) across the snowy Southern Alps – or truck north to the Marlborough wine region for heaven-sent sauvignon blanc.

Continuing north, the South Island's sunny northern flanks host the Marlborough Wine Region: quaff away long afternoons in classy winery cellar doors, and perhaps even choose to cycle between them.

ABOVE Follow bungy jumping in Queenstown with culture in Christchurch.

THE WHITE STUFF

≫→ If you're a devout powder hound or snow bunny, Queenstown has two fab ski fields to check out: the Remarkables and Coronet Peak (www.nzski.com). Coronet Peak is the only NZ field to offer night skiing, which is a magical experience under a star-filled sky. The ski season generally lasts from around June to September; the local shops are full of ski gear for purchase and hire. Even outside of the main season, heli-skiing – where you're helicoptered up to high snowy slopes in order to ski back down them – is an option for hardcore skiers (www.heliskinz.com).

The pick of the winery restaurants in Queenstown's Gibbston Wine Region is Amisfield, a jaunty stone building overlooking pretty little Lake Hayes. Amisfield's bistro does dazzling lunches, best experienced via the signature 'Trust the Chef' menu. Take your second bottle of pinot noir out to the sunny terrace. (amisfield.co.nz)

—

Milford Sound is a *looong* daytrip from Queenstown but one of the region's highlights; stay overnight in nearby Te Anau if you don't want to rush. Cruise out to see Bowen Falls, Mitre Peak, Anita Bay and Stirling Falls on a boat (realjourneys.co.nz), or take a guided kayak trip (roscosmilford kayaks.com).

DREAM DIGS

★ Once a corner store, the **Dairy** is now the pick of Queenstown's luxury B&Bs, with 13 rooms packed with classy touches such as designer bed linen and an amazing outdoor jacuzzi with eye-popping mountain views. Rates include cooked breakfasts and freshly baked afternoon teas. (www.thedairy.co.nz)

★ In Christchurch, the **George** has 53 handsomely decorated rooms within a defiantly 1970s-looking (and actually very hip) building on the fringe of Hagley Park, abutting downtown 'Chch'. Staff attend to every whim, and ritzy features include huge TVs, luxury toiletries, glossy magazines and two highly rated in-house restaurants – Pescatore and 50 Bistro. Nice one, George. (thegeorge.com)

THE HONEYMOON HANDBOOK

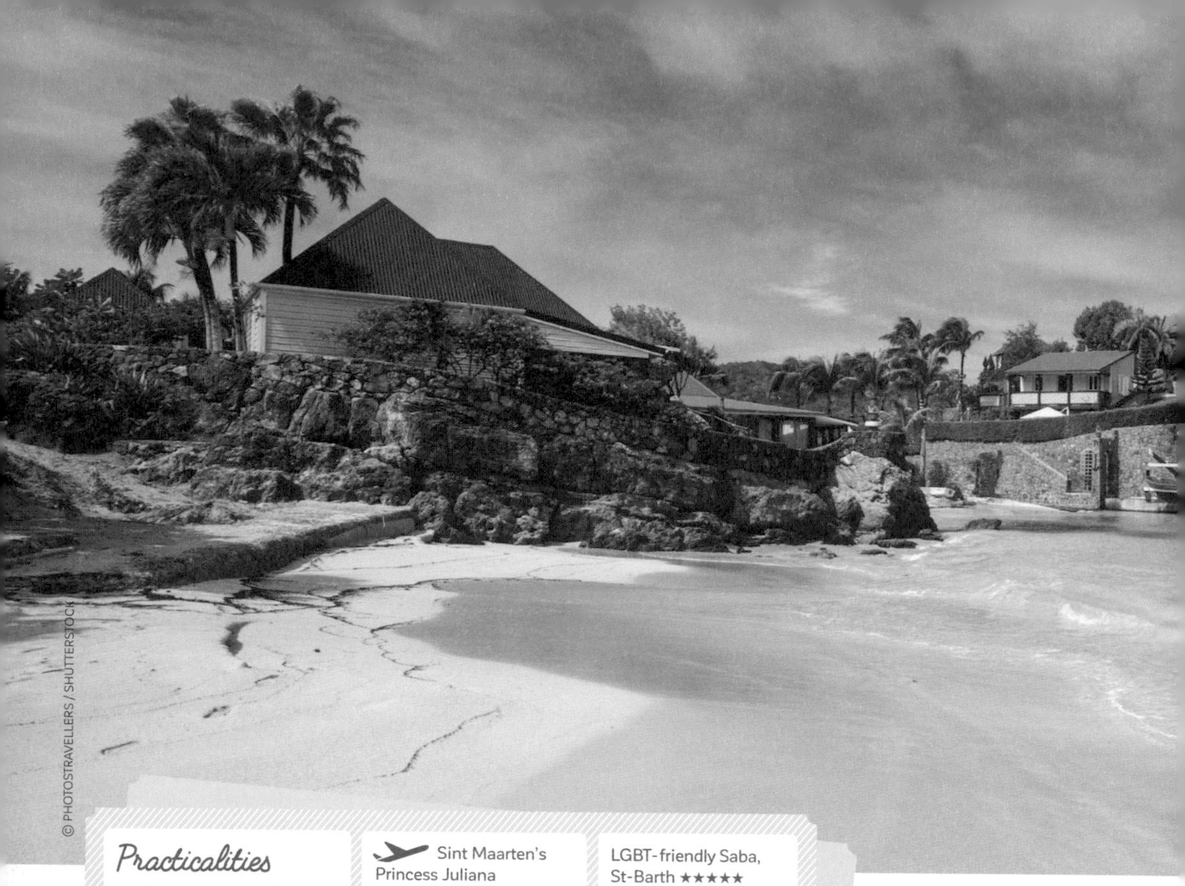

© PHOTOSTRAVELLERS / SHUTTERSTOCK

Practicalities

Make sure you have all of your sun-related toiletries before you hit the ground, as island prices are inflated.

Sint Maarten's Princess Juliana International Airport (SXM); Puerto Rico's San Juan Luis Munoz Marin International Airport (SJU)

LGBT-friendly Saba, St-Barth ★★★★★
Sint Maarten/St Martin, Puerto Rico ★★★★☆
Anguilla ★★★☆☆

(Caribbean islands that are overseas departments of European countries are generally more LGBT-friendly; same-sex marriage is legal in Saba and St Barth)

January to April is dry with low humidity; September and October are best avoided as hurricanes can sometimes blow through.

$ $

CARIBBEAN ISLAND-HOPPING

- Beach
- Relaxation
- Culture

Peach sand and azure waters, volcanic peaks and swaying palms, street-side barbecue shacks and upmarket Creole-fusion – the Leeward Islands are the Caribbean of your dreams and isles such as St-Barth, Sint Maarten/St Martin and Saba are becoming easier to hop between.

LEFT St-Barth's beaches lure the rich and famous, while Saba (below) offers incredible wildlife and jungle experiences.

© R.A.R. DE BRUIJN HOLDING BV / SHUTTERSTOCK

Gone are the days when the Caribbean was merely Honeymoon 101: a beach and beverage. Today, the popular Leeward Islands – many of them overseas territories of European countries – offer a profound sense of place that mixes local culture with the qualities of their parent countries and swirls it together with the easiness of the breeze. And this collection of islands is more accessible than ever thanks to improving inter-island boat and air transfers, meaning you can easily string together a few stops in one trip.

Consider starting in multicultural Sint Maarten/St-Martin, an island so beloved that France and the Netherlands agreed to share it. Bright foodie-friendly flavours await on the French half, and the Dutch side is your springboard to Anguilla — a scrubby limestone outcrop that has, bar none, the best beaches in the Caribbean that shimmer with an indescribable turquoise tint.

Barthélemy is the patron saint of chicness and his island spins its own brand of Antillean savoir faire – well, it is French after all! The lifestyle of the rich and famous is always on tap for those who seek it, but the quaint down-to-earth side of St-Barth lurks just beneath the bling-y veneer.

The Dutch emerald islet of Saba lacks beaches but promises a rainforest-cloaked volcano and world-renowned dive sites in their stead. The jungles that wend between settlements host incredible wildlife long forgotten on the more developed islands nearby.

THE HONEYMOON HANDBOOK

Itinerary

Fly into Sint Maarten/ St Martin and pop over to the French side for Creole-fusion fare near Grand Case and trendy beaches, such as Baie Orientale with its Euro club vibe and water sports.

≫→

Cruise down to Saba (90-minute boat ride or 10-minute flight) for diving in the national marine reserve and hiking the Santa Cruz trail.

≫→

Try the effortlessly stylish St-Barth, which promises hidden coves and a surprisingly provincial charm around small-town Lorient and Corossol.

≫→

If you have time, puddle-jump (roughly a one-hour flight) up to Puerto Rico for the Antillean version of big-city livin' in historic San Juan, then skip to Vieques next door where the bays glow with bioluminescence at night.

DIAMOND TIP

WAIT UNTIL YOU'RE ON THE GROUND TO SUSS OUT THE BEST SPOTS FOR LOCAL FARE — THEY ARE OFTEN BBQ TENTS, OR ROADSIDE OFFERINGS THAT DON'T HAVE WEBSITES.

© FRANS LEMMENS / GETTY IMAGES

© ROBERT CHIASSON / GETTY IMAGES

LEFT Hiking in Saba and the contrasting colour-pop of life in Dutch Sint Maarten.

DREAM DIGS

★ There's something undeniably aspirational about St-Barth, and the best part is discovering that beyond the nucleus of pop stars and wannabes, it's a surprisingly mellow destination. It's prime villa country too, with private digs inhabiting the bays and soaring peaks – all offering sweeping views of the sea and private pools. Choose one of the island's rental agencies instead of an online community marketplace to hook you up with a full-service abode. If you want the trappings of a hotel, go for **Le Guanahani** (www.leguanahani.com), which embraces every inch of Caribbean charm from the bright colours that bathe the wooden slatting, to the gingerbread trim and profusion of shady palms.

...AND TWO iF BY SEA

⟫⟶ Island-hopping in the Caribbean is the wave of the future, so to speak, now that the influx of tourists to the region is steadily on the upturn. Burgeoning island tourism has allowed for an increase in inter-island infrastructure with smaller airlines adding regular flights and ferries beefing up their service. Another well-connected constellation of islands is St Lucia, Martinique and Dominica, which are linked by public boat and really play up their cultural heritage and natural assets. Or, hit up the Virgin Islands (British and American) where private schooner rentals and one-resort islets are plentiful, and staunch preservation has kept much of the area's natural assets intact: the national park on St John occupies 60% of the island.

Essential Honeymoon Experiences

Charter a private boat tour to one of the smaller sandbars or empty islets orbiting any of the developed islands in the region for a romantic day trip complete with endless rum punches, fresh seafood, and miles of turquoise and blue in every direction.

—

Check out the commodity that put the Caribbean on the map: sugar-cane rum. Tastings are a fun way to get acquainted with the local culture (and not to mention quite lubricated!); some of the islands – especially the French ones – take their tipples very seriously, with flavours heavily influenced by the terroir and briny winds.

THE HONEYMOON HANDBOOK

DIAMOND TIP

RAINFOREST HIKES CAN BE MUDDY – VISIT THE MAN WITH A VAN, PARKED NEAR THE MAIN TRAILHEADS, WHO HIRES OUT WELLY BOOTS FOR A FEW TT DOLLARS.

Practicalities

 ANR Robinson
International Airport, 11km
from capital Scarborough

LGBT-friendly ★☆☆☆☆
(Homosexuality is illegal)

Take binoculars as the
birdlife is spectacular. Rain
is likely in the rainforest but
it's too hot and humid for
waterproofs – an umbrella
is better.

Temperatures are high 20°Cs/low 30°Cs
year-round. December-May is the drier season
(January-March driest).

$ $

○ Relaxation
○ Beach
◉ Culture

TOBAGO

*For a Caribbean honeymoon with idyllic beaches and a truly
local feel, this quiet island can't be beat – plus it's home to one
of the most entrancing wild adventures you can have after dark.*

Tobago is the Caribbean, but not as you think you know it. This is the region's more authentic enclave. It has the lovely beaches, yes, but without over-slickness or wall-to-wall spas. Nor does it have the industrial estates and high crime rates of its big brother island, Trinidad. It's paradise, but in a down-to-earth kind of way. That doesn't mean you can't have a heavenly honeymoon here, but it does mean that you'll know exactly where you've had it – there's no mistaking Tobago for your common-or-garden beach paradise.

The island's rugged interior is home to the world's oldest legally protected Main Ridge Forest Reserve, which in turn is home to a dazzling array of birds.

Leatherback, green and hawksbill turtles nest on the beaches of northwest Tobago from March to August; glimpsing a female lumber up the beach to lay her eggs is a moving spectacle (though be sure to do it responsibly; see sos-tobago.org). There's good diving, a smattering of historic forts and plenty of fishing villages with a pleasingly local vibe. There's also plenty of opportunities for laying under palm trees and taking sunset beach strolls.

Time your honeymoon with Trinidad & Tobago's Carnival in February/March – the biggest in the Caribbean, attended by thousands – and you can combine nature pursuits with a tremendously good fun local party or two.

BELOW Trinidad &
Tobago's February/
March Carnival is
the biggest bash in
the Caribbean.

© JO-IN DE LA BASTIDE / SHUTTERSTOCK

BELOW Pigeon Point is justifiably
famous, but best avoided if there's
a cruise ship in town.

TABLE FOR TWO

⫸⟶ Do try some local specialities while you're in Tobago, such as doubles (fried bread and chickpeas), roti and crab 'n' dumplin'. For a truly memorable meal, book Table for Two (www.tablefortwomadeforyou.com). Local chef, artist and yoga instructor Elspeth Duncan cooks up bespoke vegetarian meals for two, which you'll eat alone together on a veranda, beneath starry skies, or in a surprise location; a driver will deliver you to dinner. The chef can accommodate one couple per night, on Fridays and Saturdays only, making this a truly special one-off experience.

Ease into island life with some post-wedding beach R&R. Avoid famed Pigeon Point if there's a cruise ship in town; try quieter Bacolet Bay or a boat trip to secluded coves, with on-deck sundowners.

⫸⟶

Spend a day in the Main Ridge Forest Reserve, where trails wind amid the trees. Enlist a guide for better birdwatching.

⫸⟶

Explore the less-touristed northeast. Sail to Little Tobago, an uninhabited bird reserve, and arrange trips to world-class dive sites from the fishing village of Speyside.

⫸⟶

If it's Sunday, go to 'Sunday School': the weekly street party hosted by Buccoo village, from 8pm to the small hours.

© IAN BRIERLEY / GETTY IMAGES

TOP While away the hours in your hammock at Castara Retreats.

ABOVE Turtle-inhabited marine environments and forests that harbour hummingbirds are your reward for making it to Tobago.

DREAM DIGS

★ **Castara Retreats** is a family-run eco-hideaway on the hillside behind Castara village. Each treehouse-ish villa has ocean views, a two-person hammock and unique character. Better still, Castara is committed to working with the community – local people are employed, local businesses supported, and guests encouraged to help the fishermen haul in their catch. (castararetreats.com)

★ **Adventure Eco Villas** comprises two rustic, raised wooden cabins with little kitchens and a shared veranda, sitting within a nature reserve and tropical farm in Arnos Vale. Hummingbirds zip around the sugar feeders; after dark, bats take over. Guests are free to snack on the garden's fruit trees. (www.adventure-ecovillas.com)

Essential Honeymoon Experiences

Sail to Lovers' Bay, a beach made for honeymooners. A swish of gold and rose-pink sand segueing into calm turquoise waters, it's only accessible by boat, leaving it blissfully empty. Recruit a fisherman from Charlotteville to take you there – and pick you up again, lest you want to be marooned forever...

—

Take a stand-up paddleboarding night tour to Bon Accord Lagoon, a hotspot for glowing plankton. When you dip in your hand, the water explodes around it in bioluminescent flashes and swirls. Visit around the new moon, when skies are darkest, and it's like an aqueous aurora. (standuppaddle tobago.com)

© MARK READ / LONELY PLANET

© LEO MASON TRAVEL PHOTOS / ALAMY

© MARK READ / LONELY PLANET

DIAMOND TIP

FOR A UNIQUE HONEYMOON MEMENTO, STOP OFF IN THE FASCINATING ARTISTS' COMMUNITY OF LAS TERRAZAS (OR STAY AT THE COMMUNITY'S ECO-LUXE HOTEL MOKA) EN ROUTE TO VIÑALES TO BUY A PIECE OF ART FROM CUBAN ARTIST LESTER CAMPA AT HIS LAKESIDE STUDIO-GALLERY.

Practicalities

🧳 Leave space in your luggage for a bottle of Havana Club rum; it's ridiculously cheap and good for nostalgic mojitos when you get home.

✈ Havana

LGBT-friendly ★★★☆☆

📅 November to March is drier and cooler, but prices are higher; June to October is hot, hot, hot with a chance of hurricanes.

$ $

ABOVE The mesmerising *magote* lumps of Valle de Viñales are both mesmerising and addictive: you may not want to leave this rural retreat.

CUBA

Cuba is the Caribbean, but not as you know it. Honeymooners will love its romantic, time-warped towns, rum-fuelled music nights in Havana and Unesco-listed valleys. Best of all are the people: warm, welcoming and eager to show you the time of your life.

○ Culture
○ Adventure
○ Beach

© MARK READ / LONELY PLANET

© KAMIRA / SHUTTERSTOCK

Classic cars and faded elegance: there's nothing more romantic than a stroll down a Havana backstreet, where kids joyously swing baseball bats, lovers canoodle and a live soundtrack of rhythmic *son* accompanies free-flowing mojitos in pavement cafes and inglorious bars. Welcome to a slice of the Caribbean that time forgot.

Havana's broad boulevards, crumbling grandeur and sea-serenaded Malecón promenade, where all of city life congregates at sunset, is just the start of this honeymoon adventure. To the west of Havana you'll find Valle de Viñales, a rural backwater beloved by cyclists and climbers, famed for its world-class tobacco fields and incredible *mogotes* – towering limestone outcrops that sprout dramatically from the red earth.

To the east there's the bright lights of Varadero, a magnificent stretch of snow-white sand backed by upscale resorts. Head south and you'll find absorbing Communist propaganda at the infamous Bay of Pigs – now better known for its world-class diving than as the site of a failed US invasion. Next up are the architecturally rich cities of Cienfuegos and Trinidad, lauded by Unesco, immortalised by artists and beloved by travellers for their laidback atmospheres and pretty cobbled streets.

Along the way you'll find a unique network of heritage accommodation (many run as upmarket homestays), friendly locals and a culture quite unlike any other. Come to Cuba and you're in for one hell of a ride.

Itinerary

Start in Havana with a mojito crawl around Hemingway's old favourite haunts and a romantic stroll down the Malecón at sunset.

≫→

Splash out on hiring a vintage car (and driver) to whisk you to Viñales for some lazy days admiring the impressive

landscape from a hammock, some gentle cycling and a trip out to a tobacco plantation.

≫→

Head back east, perhaps via the Bay of Pigs for diving and Cienfuegos for a tour of its early-20th-century palaces. Don't miss photogenic Trinidad for cowboy culture, hiking

and an insight into Cuba's fascinating Santería religion.

≫→

Explore further east or head back to Havana via Varadero or one of the cayos – such as Hemingway's favourite, Cayo Guillermo – on the north coast for some classic Caribbean beach time.

LEFT Let the good times roll in Havana, where mojitos are ubiquitous and you'll no doubt find a street party or two spreading fun.

DREAM DIGS

★ **Conde de Villanueva** is a beautiful example of a restored colonial mansion in Havana's old town, with just nine luxurious bedrooms arranged around a leafy inner courtyard, complete with resident peacock. There's even an on-site cigar shop and *torcedor* (cigar roller), if you want to try one of Cuba's world-class smokes. (www.habaguanexhotels.com)

★ The term 'homestay' really doesn't do justice to the network of *casas particulares* that makes travelling through Cuba so endearing and enjoyable. Trinidad is one of the best places for sumptuous colonial *casas* – try **Colonial el Patio**, built in 1745, tastefully decorated with historic artefacts and modern art, and graced by the most exquisite, candlelit garden patio. (elpatio.trinidadhostales.com)

CHE & COMMUNISM

⟫→ Cuba's relationship with communism is complicated, fascinating and steeped in propaganda. The cult-like fame of Che Guevara lives on in street murals, billboards and museums, and the country's revolution tourism sites are well worth seeking out regardless of your political persuasion. In Havana, visit the Plaza de la Revolución – a super-sized utilitarian square where political rallies are held, looked down on by huge murals of Che and Castro; and don't miss the Museo de la Revolución, housed in the former Presidential Palace. On the Bay of Pigs, the Museo de Playa Girón is dedicated to the infamous Cold War episode that unfolded nearby in 1961 and equally unmissable.

Essential Honeymoon Experiences

Top down, a warm breeze and sun shining off the bright bonnet... there's nothing quite like a glamorous cruise around Havana in one of Cuba's legendary vintage American cars. It can cost as little as a couple of dollars for a quick chug down the seaside Malecón, or tailor-make a longer tour through Havana Super Tour (campanario63.com).

—

For a quintessential Cuban experience, take a horseback ride into the hills around Trinidad with your own private cowboy guide. A typical trip involves trotting out to the ruin-scattered Valle de los Ingenios and visiting a waterfall, where you'll have the chance to stop for a swim and a Cuba Libra under the falls.

◇

DIAMOND TIP
BEACHES IN NICARAGUA ARE PUBLIC BUT MANY ON THE PACIFIC COAST ARE ACCESSED THROUGH PRIVATE LANDS: HIRE A BOAT TO GET TO THE MOST SECLUDED PIECES OF SAND AND PARADISE.

NICARAGUA

At times unexpected, always lyrical, Nicaragua is a different side of paradise. Under the sheltering tropical sky, adventurous honeymooners can learn to surf, take a snorkelling expedition from a bejewelled Caribbean island or wander through colonial cities at sunset.

Straddling both the Caribbean and Pacific along a narrow isthmus, it's as if Nicaragua was designed for water lovers. And with the crumbling charms of its colonial centres such as Granada and León, dreadlocked nature reserves and the peaced-out Corn Islands, with sparkling white-sand beaches and world-class snorkelling, you might just rip up your tickets home.

Some of the world's best surf is found on Nicaragua's rugged Pacific Coast. There are steep point breaks for experts and plenty of easy-riding for newbies who want to try out the sport. One of the best ways to experience

LEFT Colonial churches have tales to tell in historic cities such as León and Masaya.

Nicaragua's surf scene is by staying for a week (or month!) in one of the many surf camps that offer lessons, boards, beers and bonfires... The sunsets and exclusive palm-fringed beaches are romantic and free.

For honeymooners seeking a little more luxury, there's plenty of new-spun boutique hotels, delicious colonial villas and just a touch of old-world splendour. And the best bit? Because Nicaragua only started making it onto travellers' hot lists in the past decade, much of the Central American nation retains a laid-back vibe, the exuberant culture is easy to access and shoes are not required.

© DESIGN PICS INC / ALAMY

© MARGIE POLITZER / GETTY IMAGES

Itinerary

Start your adventure in the colonial masterpiece that is Granada, where you can take handheld walks through the storied streets.

Don't miss Isla de Ometepe on your way south. You'll be rewarded with twin volcanoes, irresistible sunsets, tropical waterfalls, excellent hiking and cloud forest reserves.

»⟶

Relax on the Pacific and take some surf lessons or just sit and enjoy the view in the little surfer camps and luxurious resorts north and south of San Juan del Sur.

»⟶

Top off the trip with a flight out to the Corn Islands with authentic creole cooking, clear waters, white sands and a never-ending buzz of sweet silence.

© ANTHONY BENGER / SHUTTERSTOCK

ABOVE Volcanoes slumber across Nicaragua.

RIGHT History paves the streets of Granada – a colonial masterpiece.

© REGULA HEEB-ZWEIFEL / GETTY IMAGES

DAY-TRIPPING AROUND GRANADA

»⟶ Granada is a gem but there's just as much fun to be had outside of town, where craft villages, little lake islands, volcanoes and nature reserves are well worth exploring. For an excellent day trip, head out in the morning to Mombacho Volcano for short hikes and a zip-line canopy tour. From there, it's easy to extend your trip for artisan shopping in the Pueblos Blancos and an afternoon dip in the turquoise waters of Laguna de Apoyo. Trips can be arranged by private taxi, or book through Granada's Hotel Con Corazon (www.hotelconcorazon.com), which invests profits into local education initiatives.

NICARAGUA

108

© JANE SWEENEY / GETTY IMAGES

With its cobblestone streets, colonial churches, extravagant and sumptuous hotels, and unending terms of endearment, Granada is a highlight on many Nicaragua itineraries. After trotting through town on a romantic horse-drawn buggy ride, climb the stairs of the gorgeous Iglesia La Merced for never-ending views of the city centre at sunset.

—

With shimmering beaches and zero pretentions, Little Corn Island embodies everything a honeymoon is about. There are no cars, no roads, just a perfect beach, romantic waterfront bungalows, and miles of Caribbean Sea on every edge. An early morning dive or snorkel, followed by a creole breakfast, is an essential element of any Corn Island honeymoon.

DREAM DIGS

★ Just north of San Juan del Sur, **Mukul Resort** sits on a delicate emerald arch of private beach. This secluded retreat defines elegance and sophistication. Upgrade to one of the beach villas, which have private swimming pools and secret gardens with outdoor showers. There's good waves out front, golf, spa and access to nearby wildlife reserves. (www.mukulresort.com)

★ Travel back in time to the age of colonial opulence, marauding pirates, mystery and romance at the atmospheric **Casa del Consulado**. In the heart of Granada, this historic boutique has a delicious central pool, antique furnishings, spa treatments, and high-ceilinged cane-roof rooms. (www.hotelcasaconsulado.com)

THE HONEYMOON HANDBOOK

Practicalities

 Don't forget insect repellant, sunscreen, a driver's licence, passport, credit or debit card and light, loose-fitting clothes.

✈ Cancun is the main international gateway; if coming from the US, you can also fly into Merida.

LGBT-friendly ★★★☆☆

📅 Avoid April to June, when temperatures can reach 35°C (95°F); cooler climes prevail November to January.

$ $

○ Outdoors
○ Beach
○ Culture

YUCATÁN PENINSULA, MEXICO

Caribbean beaches, cool nature experiences, old-world colonial flavour and Maya ruins all in one fell swoop. Yes, Mexico's Yucatán is one sweet destination and there are some spectacular spots where you won't be tripping over other honeymooners.

LEFT Divers at the cenote of Chac-Mool; flamingos can be spied in the Yucatan; the fishing village of Mahahual is a low-key alternative to Cancún.

© JUSTIN FOULKES / LONELY PLANET

© LUIS JAVIER SANDOVAL / GETTY IMAGES

© CARIBBEAN / ALAMY

The Yucatán Peninsula is Mexico's top tourist draw and it certainly feels that way in Cancún and certain parts of the Riviera Maya, but you can still find many authentic spots for an intimate newly-wed getaway.

Skip the lively towns of Playa del Carmen and Tulum – packed with honeymooners – and head south for Mahahual, a laid-back fishing village that puts a premium on sustainable tourism and easy living. Mahahual captivates visitors with astonishing diving and snorkelling sites, a lovely boardwalk for evening strolls and thatched-roof restaurants whipping up the freshest of fresh seafood (don't miss Nohoch Kay). Outside town you'll find secluded white-sand beaches for some blissful alone time.

Spice things up with a road trip to cultural capital Mérida, a dreamy colonial city known for its thriving culinary scene, world-class Maya history museum (www.granmuseodelmundomaya.com.mx) and atmospheric historic centre lined with elegant mansions: this is a side of Mexico that you won't see on the Riviera. The city makes a great base from which to explore Maya ruins, cenotes (limestone sinkholes) and the biosphere reserve of Celestún, where you can spy flamingos during boat tours.

THE HONEYMOON HANDBOOK

Drive south of Cancún to the tranquil fishing village of Mahahual, plunge into azure Caribbean waters at biosphere reserve Banco Chinchorro, explore remote beaches south of Mahahual and dine on the sand by candlelight.

≫→

Head northwest to the Yucatán's cultural capital, Mérida. Visit the Maya museum, try regional cuisine at La Chaya Maya (lachayamaya.com), then let loose with mezcals and tropical music in *cantina* La Negrita.

≫→

Venture east of Mérida to explore mysterious Maya ruins and limestone sinkholes, before heading north to spend a night in an 18th-century hacienda.

≫→

Set aside time for Celestún, a refreshingly low-key beach town where surrounding mangroves are home to a large flamingo colony.

DIAMOND TIP

WHEN VISITING SMALL TOWNS LIKE CELESTÚN AND MAHAHUAL, BRING CASH. ATMS OFTEN RUN OUT OF CASH AND MANY PLACES DON'T ACCEPT PLASTIC.

© JUSTIN FOULKES / LONELY PLANET

©OLE STEFFENSEN / 500PX

LEFT Beyond Cancún, fishing villages such as Punta Allen show the wilder, less touristy, heart of the Yucatan Peninsula; the pyramids of Chichén Itzá.

DREAM DIGS

★ Nothing says romance *a la Mexicana* like a stay in an 18th-century hacienda, and **Xcanatún** ranks among the best of them. The suites, decked out with exquisite rustic furnishings, were made for chillaxing (sorry, no TVs but we're guessing you won't need one) and the award-winning onsite restaurant rocks. (www.xcanatun.com)

★ Mahahual in general doesn't do ultra-luxurious – and therein lies its charm. **Ko'ox Quinto Sole**'s minimalist rooms are certainly comfy enough, but what makes this place special is its delightful swimmable beach and sweeping ocean views of the Mexican Caribbean – assuming you splurge on waterfront digs, which you most definitely should. (www.kooxquinto soleboutiquehotel.com)

The Maya saw *cenotes* and their subterranean river systems as gateways to the underworld. But a honeymoon to the underworld is a hard sell, so think of them simply as gorgeous swimming holes. You'll find many in and around Valladolid, including a spectacular one at Hacienda San Lorenzo Oxman (facebook.com/haciendasanlorenzoo).

The Yucatán boasts some of the most impressive pre-Hispanic structures you'll ever lay eyes on. Chichén Itzá is the best restored, but most crowded; Tulum (also crowded) has the most dramatic location, perched on a rocky outcrop above turquoise sea; Ek Balam is the place to go to share a quiet moment together atop a 32m-high pyramid.

ESCAPE TO CELESTÚN

⟫→ For a glorious nature experience, head 100km west of Mérida to the sunbaked fishing village of Celestún. Even non-birders get a kick out of boat tours into the mangroves, where you can see flamingos doing their thing in a protected biosphere reserve. Consider staying a night or two at Casa de Celeste Vida (www.hotelcelestevida.com), a friendly family-run guesthouse where you usually have the whole beach to yourself. If you want a more personalised tour of the mangroves, your hosts can arrange outings with Celestun's foremost experts on the area's wildlife. *This* is the quiet escape you've been dreaming about.

DIAMOND TIP

IF YOU'D RATHER KEEP YOUR PACKING LIST DOWN, HAULOVER BEACH IN MIAMI MAY BE THE MOST FAMOUS CLOTHING OPTIONAL STRIP OF SAND IN THE USA.

It's very laid-back here, but some of the fancier establishments have dress codes; check when booking and, to be safe, pack something smart for high-end dining.

✈ Miami International Airport (MIA) or Fort Lauderdale-Hollywood International Airport (FLL).

LGBT-friendly ★★★★★

The shoulder season – late March to May – is perfect if you want to avoid big crowds, high season prices and the possibility of hurricanes.

$ $

○ Culture
○ Beach
◉ Food & Drink

MiAMi &
SOUTH FLORiDA, USA

If sexiness, beauty, fun and relaxation are the components of a good honeymoon, few destinations exude these qualities quite like South Florida. Neon-drenched hotels, white-sand beaches, destination dining and one of the biggest wetlands in North America awaits.

Sultry and semi-tropical Miami struts its stuff at the crossroads of Latin America and the Caribbean, juking from the cool art deco district of South Beach to the Mediterranean-inspired mansions of Coral Gables and the hipster arts scene of Wynwood. In between are European expats browsing art galleries and skyscrapers glittering over restaurants that range from four-star to delicious dive. Then there's the Cuban Americans slapping dominoes at pickup games in parks, models on photo shoots and, of course, miles of sugary beachfront.

Miami is a city that can fulfil every glamorous honeymoon whim and knows how to have a good time. Here you can kick back to the beat of house DJs or live Cuban music, polishing off your rum with a view of the sun bleeding into Biscayne Bay, a night of intense clubbing, or tapas in a lounge that specialises in Catalonian cuisine.

Further south are the Everglades, an enormous

LEFT The palm-fronted art deco district of South Beach is a national historic site.

© PHOTOSVIT / GETTY IMAGES

ABOVE Take a boat out around South Beach.

Itinerary

Start in Miami – well, Miami Beach. Do a walking tour of the art deco district and lounge out on the sugary white sand. Enjoy some waterside club-hopping and have a romantic meal in a glitzy hotel or a Cuban diner.

≫→

Head to Wynwood and the Design District, soaking up nightlife and new restaurants in Miami's bohemian arts district.

≫→

Drive down to the Everglades and take a tour of miles of sawgrass prairie and alligator-prowled swamps.

≫→

Roadtrip all along the Overseas Highway to the colourful, Caribbean town of Key West – a floating enclave of galleries, outdoor cafes and tropical bars.

natural park that contains a wonderland of sawgrass prairie and alligator-prowled swamps. Further south still, amid the teal waters of Florida Bay and the Gulf of Mexico, is the archipelago of the Florida Keys forming a necklace of mangrove-cloaked islands, strung together by spectacular US Highway 1 – the Overseas Highway – which terminates amid the pretty historic neighbourhoods and wild parties of Key West.

RIGHT South Florida isn't just about the Miami party – take time out to explore the Everglades and Florida Keys archipelago, too.

GLIDING OVER THE KEYS

≫→ For a road trip with a difference, rent a car and drive down to Key West. From Miami it's four hours non-stop driving, but to do the drive justice spend longer – this is a trip to savour. The Overseas Highway crosses the sapphire-and-cerulean waters of Florida Bay and the Gulf of Mexico, hitting more than 100 'Keys' – islands – along the way. Each has its own character, but the eccentricities of this odd archipelago all get shaken into a cocktail for the ages in Key West. Here, among colonial Caribbean homes, you'll find art galleries, fine dining, and a population that loves an outdoor drink.

© NO_LIMIT_PICTURES / GETTY IMAGES

© MATT MUNRO / LONELY PLANET

Take a walking tour of Miami Beach's art deco district and marvel at the neon retro glam. Grab grub in hip Wynwood, then back to the beach for cocktails on Ocean Avenue. Finish the evening by strolling into one of the area's grand hotels, such as the Delano, Shore Club or Raleigh, where you can lounge by an enormous pool.

—

Strap on some waterproof boots and head down to the Everglades for a tour of the wilds. You can go the conventional route, via a kayak, or arrange a 'wet walk' – a wade into a local cypress dome. Doesn't sound romantic? You'll be surrounded by cooing wildlife and a jungle of blooming flowers.

DREAM DIGS

★ The **Shore Club** is one of the newer generation of South Beach mega hotels, but it still feels like it's landed from the future: the minimalist rooms are decked out in a white palette so cool it's like snow, surrounded by tropical landscaped gardens and shimmering pools. (www.morganshotelgroup.com)

★ If the Shore Club is stripped down, **The Pelican** is an outrageous riot of colour and experience. Each of the 30 rooms is highly individualised from psychedelic '60s to zebra (really. Zebra). It's a playful spot with great access to the beach and the human parade that is Ocean Drive. (www.pelicanhotel.com)

© RELIGIOUS IMAGES / GETTY IMAGES

© CHRIS HEPBURN / GETTY IMAGES

© FRANCESCO RICCARDO IACOMINO / 500PX

Practicalities

💼 Bring glam nightclub-worthy outfits for Las Vegas, but river sandals and comfy outdoor sportswear for national parks and road-tripping.

✈ McCarran International Airport, Las Vegas, Nevada

📅 Late April, May, September and early October bring milder temperatures to the desert and little or no snow.

$ $

LGBT-friendly ★★★☆☆
(Las Vegas is a premier gay honeymoon destination. However, some conservative, religious and rural areas of the Southwest remain intolerant.)

ABOVE A roadtrip to the arid dreamscape of Utah's Monument Valley can be combined with a quickie wedding or glitzy honeymoon in Vegas (left).

DiAMONO TiP

FOR LODGING, RIVER RAFTING, MULE RIDES AND BACKPACKING iN GRAND CANYON NATIONAL PARK, BOOK UP TO 13 MONTHS iN AOVANCE.

LAS VEGAS & SOUTHWEST USA

○ Outdoors
◉ Adventure
○ Culture

Better known for its quickie weddings, Las Vegas is also a surprisingly sophisticated honeymoon destination with an ubercool urban vibe. It's also a gateway city for a romantic road trip of a lifetime through the Southwest's canyon country and deserts – no roughing it required.

© LUCKY-PHOTOGRAPHER / GETTY IMAGES

Wild river rafting, epic hikes and canyoneering, rugged 4WD routes to ancient Native American sites, national park lodges and ranch resorts will fill up a week, two weeks or a whole month on your honeymoon journey through the US Southwest. This trip is for couples who believe that romantic solitude under starry skies is just as good as turn-down service with a chocolate on the pillow.

Your jumping-off point is Las Vegas, Nevada. A quick city break lets you both be pampered and have around-the-clock fun – it's the perfect way to decompress after a big wedding. Once you've rested up, it's time to hop in the car for an epic road trip, starting at the Grand Canyon, an unmatched natural wonder in the nearby state of Arizona.

Next up on the Southwest's greatest-hits list are southern Utah's spectacular national parks, which run from river-cut Zion Canyon to the natural sandstone formations of Arches, outside the four-seasons adventure hub of Moab. Meanwhile down in New Mexico, the charming adobe buildings, art galleries and hot springs of Santa Fe and Taos await.

And don't miss a visit to some of the Southwest's tribal lands. In Monument Valley, you can go horseback riding with a Navajo guide among towering sandstone buttes, made famous by Hollywood westerns.

Itinerary

≫⟶ Overnight or spend a weekend in Las Vegas, a buzzing casino-resort city in Nevada's desert, to start (or end) your trip with a bang.

≫⟶ Take a day or overnight trip to Arizona's Grand Canyon, via either the popular, easily accessible South Rim or the more peaceful and remote North Rim.

≫⟶ Hire a convertible car or a 4WD Jeep to road trip through southern Utah's spectacular national parks for up to a week.

≫⟶ With extra time and unlimited miles on your rental car, detour into New Mexico, especially for Southwestern fusion cuisine, art, culture and history in Santa Fe.

LEFT Take at least a day to soak up the Grand Canyon, otherwise you might miss sights like the Havasu Falls, hidden within it.

DREAM DIGS

★ For the ultimate escape, make your way to the one-of-a-kind **Amangiri** resort. Hidden in the canyon country of southern Utah, this intimate boutique property is the perfect getaway destination or stopover. Suites have their own outdoor lounge and fireplace, and some come with a private plunge pool. At sunrise, launch in a hot-air balloon for views of the valley's dazzling rock formations. Cap off each day with a seasonal, sustainable Southwestern feast for two on the terrace. (www.aman.com/resorts/amangiri)

LAS VEGAS WEDDINGS

⟫⟶ Getting hitched in Vegas is a cinematic cliché, but it's also totally fun. When wedding planning starts to feel like work, you may just be tempted to elope. Every year, thousands of couples tie the knot in Sin City's wedding chapels, many with an Elvis impersonator serenading them. But Vegas offers more upmarket destination weddings, too, from outdoor ceremonies in strikingly beautiful places like Red Rock Canyon to sophisticated shindigs at casino resorts on the Strip, such as the Bellagio with its artificial lake and dancing fountains. Remember to apply for a marriage licence in advance (yes, you do need one: *The Hangover* experience is a myth); visit www.clarkcountynv.gov/clerk/services/Pages/MarriageLicenses.aspx for details.

Essential Honeymoon Experiences

The Grand Canyon is the most-visited attraction in the Southwest, but you can't experience its majesty during a brief roadside stop. Spend at least a day at the national park, catching sunrise and sunset from the canyon rim or the Colorado River, reachable by foot, mule or river raft.

—

In Las Vegas, the neon-lit Strip is both glamorous and wonderfully kitsch. Find non-stop thrills day and night, not only at casino gaming tables but at restaurants, nightspots and attractions up and down Las Vegas Blvd. Whether you spend a hundred or a thousand dollars a day, it's always entertaining.

DiAMOND TiP

PRE-ORDER A FLOWER-LEI GREETING FOR BOTH OF YOU UPON ARRIVAL AT THE AIRPORT FROM GREETERS OF HAWAII (WWW. GREETERSOFHAWAII.COM).

Practicalities

 Honolulu International Airport, O'ahu

🧳 A compact, waterproof or underwater camera lets you capture fun at the beach and snorkelling with tropical fish.

📅 You can visit Hawaii year-round, though the driest months with the calmest ocean conditions are May to October.

LGBT- friendly ★★★★★
(Hawaii's biggest LGBT scene revolves around Waikiki Beach on O'ahu. Maui, Kaua'i and the Big Island have low-key local communities.)

$ $ – $ $ $

○ Beach
◉ Relaxation
○ Outdoors

HAWAii

The Hawaiian Islands are a classic honeymoon destination, where you could happily laze on the beach all day, every day. But if you're an adventurous couple, Hawaii's volcanoes, rain forests, protected parks and spectacular coral reefs should also tempt you.

Made up of the most geographically remote islands on the planet, the Hawaiian archipelago belongs as much to Polynesia as it does to the USA. In Hawaii, honeymooners will find wide sweeps of white, black and golden sands, famous surf breaks and aquamarine bays perfect for snorkelling and diving. Take a romantic sunset cruise off Waikiki Beach or an all-day catamaran sail along Kaua'i's Na Pali Coast, where you can peer up at towering sea cliffs as dolphins and sea turtles swim nearby. In winter, whale-watching boat trips to spot migratory humpbacks in the national marine sanctuary are a must-do on Maui.

Even if you're more of a landlubber than a water baby, Hawaii's main islands offer fantastic scenic drives, such as Maui's jungly road to Hana, Chain of Craters Rd through the Big Island's Hawai'i Volcanoes National Park, and epic sea-to-summit drives to the top of Haleakala and Mauna Kea volcanoes. Hawaii also preserves its *paniolo* (cowboy) heritage at historic ranches on the main islands, where you can go horseback riding, ride a zip line or take a guided tour of sites where Hollywood TV and movie blockbusters including *Jurassic Park* and *Lost* were filmed.

LEFT The Na Pali Coast (top) and Waikiki Beach.

© MATT MUNRO / LONELY PLANET

© DAVE FLEETHAM / GETTY IMAGES

HAWAiiAN LUAUS

⟫⟶ Hip-shaking dancers, endless buffets and tiki drinks – what's not to love about a Hawaiian luau? Most commercial luau in the islands are seriously overpriced. The stage shows can be lackluster or even tacky, and are often accompanied by watered-down cocktails and bland food. A shining exception is Maui's **Old Lahaina Luau** (www.oldlahainaluau.com), filled with authentic Hawaiian hula dancing, music, chanting and storytelling, as well as above-average island dishes. For locals, having a luau means celebrating a special occasion like a baby's first birthday with the *'ohana* (extended family and friends) – you'd be very lucky to get an invitation to one.

Itinerary

The islands of Kaua'i and Maui are the top honeymoon destinations with oceanfront hotels and lush tropical scenery. Base yourself in one place for a week, then make day trips around the island you've picked. With two weeks, visit both.

⟫⟶

For outdoor adventures and wilder landscapes, fly over to Hawai'i the Big Island. Check into a Kona or Kohala coast resort for a few days, then circle the island from hidden beaches to volcanic peaks.

⟫⟶

If you crave shopping, restaurants and big-city buzz, tack on a few days at Honolulu's Waikiki Beach on the island of O'ahu.

© EDDY GALEOTTI / SHUTTERSTOCK

LEFT Waikiki Beach is your classic surfers' paradise, but there's also plenty of big-city buzz.

© MATT MUNRO / LONELY PLANET

ABOVE & RIGHT Traditional island foods include roast pork, taro and syrupy shaved ice.

© MATT MUNRO / LONELY PLANET

It was ancient Hawaiians who invented the sport of what they called *he'e nalu* (wave sliding). Surfing lessons and rentals are easy to find at popular beaches around the main islands, especially on the surf-centric North Shores of O'ahu, Maui and Kaua'i. The biggest swells arrive during the wet season (December to March).

—

Hawaiian music is the heartbeat of the islands, and hula dancing is their soul. The best place to experience either is at an island festival or neighbourhood community centre. In Honolulu, Waikiki Beach hosts fantastic, free live music and hula shows by island performers. Check staradvertiser.com to find out about events.

DREAM DiGS

★ Although you might be skeptical that a worldwide luxury chain could offer an authentic sense of place, the **Four Seasons Resort Hualalai** on the Big Island's Kona coast does. It's not just the fresh tropical flowers and Hawaiiana everywhere you look, or the sophisticated cuisine made from sustainably sourced, local ingredients at 'Ulu Ocean Grill. It's also the resort's eco-friendly practices and island conservation projects, and its Ka'upulehu Cultural Center, where you can meet Hawaiian artists and *kupuna* (elders). Afterward, you can still luxuriate in a coconut scrub at the spa or take a dip in the infinity pool. (www.fourseasons.com/hualalai)

Practicalities

✈ Calgary, Alberta

LGBT-friendly ★★★★★

 Mountain weather is extremely changeable, so pack layers (warm base, fleece, waterproof shell), hat and gloves – even in summer.

📅 July to early October for hiking, climbing and other summer activities; December to March for skiing, dogsledding and winter adventures.

$ $

○ Outdoors
◉ Adventure
○ Relaxation

ROCKIES, CANADA

Whether you travel in summer or winter, the glacier-topped peaks, bubbling hot springs and blue-green lakes of Canada's Rocky Mountains create a dramatic backdrop for an active honeymoon – with plenty of scope for added luxuries.

LEFT Pin-up Moraine Lake has to be one of the world's best settings for a romantic lodge.

LEFT & ABOVE Frozen canyons become adventure playgrounds in winter; man dressed in full Siksika tribal attire.

With vast stretches of protected parkland, Western Canada's Rocky Mountain region is an immense outdoor playground. The marquee destinations are Banff and Jasper National Parks, where you can explore glaciers, canoe across turquoise lakes, and wend your way along wooded hiking trails; Banff alone has more than 1,600km of hiking paths. But plenty of other adventures await and some lodges offer special services, such as a private butler, couple's massage, or breakfast in bed, to add a touch of luxury.

Paddle together along the blue-green waters of Emerald Lake in Yoho National Park, and refresh lakeside with cured elk and a craft beer. Hike to a teahouse overlooking the glaciers above Lake Louise, where you can share a slice of freshly baked chocolate cake, or test your climbing skills together on Banff's Via Ferrata, a spectacular guided route that uses fixed anchors and metal cables to allow novice climbers to experience a thrilling mountain ascent. Ogle the peaks along the Icefields Parkway, one of Canada's great drives, then soak in natural hot springs and cuddle in a secluded mountaintop suite or lakeside lodge.

Prefer a snow-capped holiday? The Rockies abound with ski and snowboard resorts, and many hiking paths become snowshoeing routes in winter. Strap on ice cleats to hike through dramatic canyons where rivers and waterfalls freeze into walls of sculpted ice. Or snuggle by the fire with a hot drink and watch the snowflakes fall.

THE HONEYMOON HANDBOOK

Itinerary

Start in the town of Banff, located within the national park, to check out its small museums, cosy pubs and local restaurants serving bison burgers and fresh trout. See a concert or play at the arts-focused Banff Centre.

≫→

Take your holiday snapshots along the shores of Lake Louise, and spend at least a day exploring the waterfalls, lakes, and trails in Yoho National Park.

≫→

Drive the spectacular Icefields Parkway, where you can stop and hike to the glaciers.

≫→

In more remote Jasper, go river rafting, take a motorcycle tour through the mountains, or continue putting those hiking boots to good use.

DIAMOND TIP

EXPLORE THE REGION'S ABORIGINAL CULTURE: BOOK A SWEAT LODGE CEREMONY AT NATIVE-OWNED CROSS RIVER WILDERNESS CENTRE (WWW.CROSSRIVER.CA) OR ATTEND A FIRST NATIONS POWWOW.

© JUSTIN FOULKES / LONELY PLANET

© PHOTOGRAPHER / IMAGE LIBRARY

OREAM DiGS

★ Wake to wraparound mountain views in your private suite atop the gondola station at **Kicking Horse Mountain Resort**. At the Eagle's Eye (2,345m), with just two simple but comfortable mountaintop units, you and your beloved can lodge in romantic seclusion, with a personal butler to pamper you and a private chef to prepare your meals. In winter, your private ski guide will show you the best runs as you make the first tracks in untouched powder. (www.kickinghorseresort.com)

★ Or choose a lakeview suite at secluded **Moraine Lake Lodge**, a rustically elegant off-the-grid escape offering guided hiking, leisurely canoeing, and upscale dining: no kids under eight allowed. (www.morainelake.com)

ROMANCE BY RAIL

⫸→ To combine your mountain adventure with time by the sea or in the city on Canada's west coast, consider starting your trip in Vancouver, then taking the train to the Rockies. Via Rail (www.viarail.ca), Canada's national rail carrier, travels overnight from Vancouver to Jasper. Book a cosy cabin for two and you'll wake as the train begins its climb into the mountains. Or if your budget allows, travel on the Rocky Mountaineer (www.rockymountaineer.com), a luxury private rail service that offers several routes between the coast and Banff, Lake Louise, or Jasper, along with optional guided tours and outdoor experiences.

Essential Honeymoon Experiences

If you're travelling during the colder months, book a quintessential Canadian adventure: a dogsledding tour through the national parks. You'll learn how the guides care for their dogs and how to guide the team yourself as you cruise between snowy pines and along lakeshores. (kingmik dogsledtours.com)

—

Wrap up your outdoor adventures with a relaxing soak in a mineral pool. Banff, Jasper, and Kootenay National Parks all have public hot springs, but for a more luxe experience, schedule a couple's massage and soak at the grand Fairmont Banff Springs Hotel, where three hot pools with waterfalls surround a mineral spa. (fairmont.com/banff-springs)

THE HONEYMOON HANDBOOK

DIAMOND TIP

HIRE A 4WD CAR AND MAKE SURE YOU STOP TO FILL UP AND CHECK TYRES REGULARLY AS THERE'S NO ROADSIDE ASSISTANCE.

ARGENTINA
RUTA
40

Practicalities

 Buenos Aires

🧳 Sunglasses, large refillable water carriers, face wipes and an epic playlist. It's a long (and sometimes dusty) road...

📅 September to November (spring) is generally the best time to visit Argentina. In January, Easter and July national holidays push up demand and prices for transport and accommodation.

$ $ – $ $ $

LGBT-friendly ★★★★☆
Same-sex marriage is legal and Buenos Aires and other big cities are liberal, but Argentina is still a largely traditional Catholic society in rural areas.

⭕ Adventure
⭕ Food & Drink
⭕ Culture

ARGENTINA

Desert moonscapes, Andean peaks and cowboy life are just the tip of the iceberg along Ruta 40 – a long-distance highway running deep into Argentine Patagonia. For newly-weds with a sense of adventure, this could be the most romantic steak-and-wine-fuelled road trip in the world.

Ruta 40 runs parallel to the Andes and stretches 5000km from the Bolivian border at La Quiaca to the Cabo Virgenes on the southern coast of Argentina. It's an epic route that could take many, many weeks to drive, but less time-rich adventurers can have just as much fun on a fly-and-drive combo instead – treating the road as the backbone to your perfect, tailor-made trip.

If you've got a few weeks for your honeymoon, an ideal abridged version could take in Salta, the northern deserts and the Jujuy mountains; the award-winning

wine region of Mendoza; the lush forests and crystal clear lakes around Bariloche; and the stunning glaciers and snow-covered mountains around El Chalten in Patagonia. Fly between major cities and hire a car to explore the most spectacular sections of the route, giving you time to enjoy some delightful detours along the way – such as a trip inland to experience life on a traditional *estancia* in Córdoba's Sierras Chicas mountains.

Starting your adventure in Buenos Aires and flying into gateway cities such as Salta, Mendoza and Bariloche also gives you

LEFT AND BELOW Tango and empanadas (delicious fried pockets of stuffed pastry).

LEFT On the Viedma Glacier in Argentine Patagonia; Ruta 40 runs for 5000km down the spine of Argentina.

Begin your trip in Buenos Aires, admiring its colonial architecture and colourful streets. Enjoy Palermo's stylish restaurants and San Telmo's bohemian bars.

≫→

Fly to the historic cathedral city of Salta to enjoy traditional culture, music and dance.

≫→

Drive north to explore Jujuy's mountain range, then south of Salta to Cafayate's high-altitude vineyards.

≫→

Head west either to the wineries of Mendoza or to Bariloche, a great base to explore the Nahuel Huapi National Park in the foothills of the Patagonian Andes.

≫→

Hire a car and drive south on Ruta 40 via the cave paintings at Cueva de las Manos, the Perito Moreno Glacier, Cerro Chalten and down to El Calafate.

a chance to mix outdoors pursuits with the unique culture, vibrant nightlife, revered restaurants and boutique hotels of Argentina's historic cities: the perfect contrast to life on the road where you'll find only nature's changing scenery, each other and your car for company.

© MATT MUNRO / LONELY PLANET

LEFT & ABOVE Argentina is famed for its high-altitude vineyards; colourful La Boca, a suburb of vivacious Buenos Aires.

LIFE ON THE ROAD

≫→ A road trip is the most romantic and rewarding way to explore Argentina but it's also a real commitment. Only attempt it if you're both experienced drivers and contented passengers. Plan your stops and book accommodation in advance, ensure you always have a full tank of fuel and pack plenty of water for long stretches. With most main roads now tarmacked, it's possible to motor along at thrilling speeds with the wind in your hair, but mountain roads are often just gravel paths and that means teeth-chattering bumpiness at 10km an hour. For newly-weds with a sense of adventure, it's the perfect initiation into married life.

© JO-IN W BANAGAN / GETTY IMAGES

Essential Honeymoon Experiences

The otherworldly drive north of Salta into the mountainous Jujuy province is breathtaking. Highlights include the 'hill of seven colours'– a geological marvel 600 million years in the making – and the moon-like Salinas Grandes salt flats.

—

Life on a traditional ranch is a quintessential Argentine experience and there are plenty of family-run estancias in the wine regions of Cafayate, Cordoba and Mendoza. Watch gauchos round up cattle on horseback, ride out across lush plains, feast on campfire-roasted beef and drink red wine as the sun sets. Then cosy up under the night sky, mesmerised by the infinite beauty of the Milky Way.

DREAM DIGS

★ Situated in Córdoba's Sierras Chicas, stunning poolside scenery, delicious food and award-winning wine come as standard at **Estancia Los Potreros**. But what's special about this family-run estancia is the relaxed hospitality, stylish décor and hammocks on the candlelit terrace, accompanied by whinnying foals at your window in the mornings. (estancialospotreros.com)

★ Lakeside **Aguas Arriba Lodge** is an exclusive Patagonian eco-lodge inside the Glaciers National Park. Perfectly camouflaged by the forest, with access only by boat, it's paradise for wildlife lovers. With majestic views of Mt Fitz Roy, Mt Torre and the Vespignani Glacier, couples can fish, climb and hike or just relax and enjoy being at one with each other in nature. (www.aguasarribalodge.com)

THE HONEYMOON HANDBOOK

Practicalities

💼 The equatorial sun is strong – a hat and high-factor sun screen are essential. Consider hiring/packing a shortie wetsuit so you can snorkel for longer (because it's so amazing!), even if the water is colder.

✈ Flights from Quito and Guayaquil (mainland Ecuador) fly into Baltra or San Cristobál

📅 July to November – cooler, drier, rougher seas. December to June – wetter, but calmer, better for snorkelling (warmer, better visibility). Wildlife highlights vary year-round.

$ $ $

LGBT-friendly ★★☆☆☆
(Homosexuality was only made legal in 1997 and Ecuador has a conservative Catholic society)

ABOVE Sea turtles and blue-footed boobies are some of the residents you're likely to encounter on a trip to Darwin's islands.

DIAMOND TIP

PRONE TO SEASICKNESS? LOWER DECK CABINS ON A MEDIUM OR LARGE SHIP ARE USUALLY MOST STABLE; SEAS ARE ROUGHEST AUGUST TO SEPTEMBER.

GALÁPAGOS, ECUADOR

Dolphins playing in the bow waves, unique animals wandering close enough to touch, birds acting amorously, the sun setting into the endless ocean – few trips are as memorable as a cruise around this remote Pacific archipelago off Ecuador.

○ Outdoors
◉ Adventure
○ Beach

Itinerary

≫→ After a two-hour flight from the mainland, set sail right away. Cruises usually last four or eight days; eight is better.

≫→ Landing sites visited depend on your vessel. They might include the blinding-white sand and sea lions of Gardner Bay (Española), the piles of marine iguanas at Punta Espinosa (Fernandina), or Tagus Cove (Isabela), where Darwin stepped ashore.

≫→ A typical Galápagos day? Breakfast, a shore-landing, a guided nature walk; lunch back on board followed by a second landing elsewhere; maybe snorkelling or kayaking; back to the boat for drinks and dinner; and a briefing on where you're heading next.

© WESTEND61 / GETTY IMAGES

© ANDRE DISTEL PHOTOGRAPHY / GETTY IMAGES

Waved albatrosses mate for life. When the males return to the Galápagos isle of Española in March, they await their partners; when the females arrive, pairs perform complex courtships – like a feathered flamenco – bowing, swaying, jousting with their beaks. It's one of Mother Nature's most romantic sights. And just one of many reasons why this remote archipelago is ideal for a honeymoon.

Strewn 1000km off mainland Ecuador, and made famous by Darwin's revolutionary evolutionary thinking, the Galápagos Islands are unique. Many of the animals are endemic, and unfeasibly tame. Marine iguanas, Galápagos tortoises,

Galápagos penguins, blue-footed boobies... Wildlife-loving newly-weds will be in heaven.

There are 13 main islands, best navigated by cruise. Vessels range from 100-passenger ships (more impersonal, more stable) to 12-berth sailboats (more intimate, more rocky). Choose which suits your style: a cabin with balcony on a bigger boat, for private sunsets? Or perhaps a small yacht with billowing sails seems more romantic? Each boat follows a set itinerary to prevent crowding, so if you have a particular interest – flamingo lagoons, fur seal hang-outs, volcano hikes, human history – pick your cruise based on route. Though every Galápagos journey will be a magical one.

LEFT Stalk flamingo lagoons for flock sightings, then snorkel in the clear waters at Isabela island.

DREAM DIGS

★ Follow in glamorous footsteps aboard the **M/Y Grace**: Prince Rainier of Monaco and Grace Kelly honeymooned on this historic motor yacht in the 1950s; now restored, she has nine luxurious cabins, an on-deck jacuzzi, wine cellar, alfresco dining area, second-to-none food and service, and two naturalist guides aboard. (quasarex.com)

★ If you prefer a land-based Galápagos trip, try the **Galápagos Safari Camp** – nine safari-style tents tucked into Santa Cruz's lush, bird-rife highlands. There's an infinity pool, classy lounge-bar and plenty of activities on offer, such as horse trekking and diving, plus forays to other islands. (galapagos safaricamp.com)

CABIN FEVER

➤➤➤ Worried about being cooped up on a boat with other people for your whole honeymoon? Counter-intuitively, bigger boats can offer more privacy – tables for two rather than communal dining, for instance. Also consider bolting on extra days of quality time together at the end of your cruise on the Ecuadorian mainland. Include a few days in colonial Quito, perhaps staying at elegant converted mansion, Casa Gangotena (www.casagangotena.com); from here you can head south along the Avenue of the Volcanoes or north into the cloud forest. For more wildlife indulgence and a real adventure, fly to a remote community-run eco-lodge in the Ecuadorian Amazon, such as luxurious Sacha Lodge (www.sachalodge.com).

Take every opportunity to jump into the Galápagos's wildlife-rich waters, particularly to snorkel with playful sea lions, who will twist and twirl around you; look for penguins, turtles and marine iguanas, too. Punta Vicente Roca (Isabela Island) and James Bay (Santiago Island) are good snorkel spots.

—

Homesick whalers used to deposit love letters at Post Office Bay in Floreana and visitors can still do the same; passing ships would pick up the mail and deliver it – sometimes years later. To prolong your honeymoon, leave a self-addressed note here, and see how long it takes someone to deliver it back to you.

DIAMOND TIP

ASSEMBLE A CLASSIC FRENCH PICNIC OF BAGUETTES, CHEESE, FRUIT AND VEGGIES AT AMBOISE'S RENOWNED SUNDAY FOOD MARKET; BRING A LOIRE WINE.

○ Culture
◑ Food & Drink
○ Outdoors

PARIS & THE LOIRE VALLEY, FRANCE

For sheer romance and magic, France can't be beat. Split your time between the City of Light and the châteaux, villages and vineyards of the Loire Valley.

For centuries, the sparkling city of Paris has attracted artists, intellectuals and lovers in search of romance in all its forms: what better way to start your honeymoon? Parks such as the Jardin du Luxembourg, with their flower beds and ponds, are ideal for a dreamy stroll. To stimulate your mind and imagination, the city has world-renowned museums – the Louvre, of course, but also smaller gems; Parisians' personal favourites often include the Musée Rodin and Musée Picasso. Colourful food markets, such as the one along the Latin Quarter's Rue Mouffetard, offer a cornucopia of the finest French edibles – perfect for a deluxe picnic for two.

For dinner, dress up and indulge in traditional French cuisine.

Three hours south of Paris, the verdant Loire Valley provides the perfect change of pace. One-time playground of kings and queens, the area is home to many of France's most magnificent châteaux, some of them medieval fortresses redolent of knights, others Renaissance pleasure palaces with soaring cupolas and glittering banquet halls. Among them, ancient villages produce excellent wines you can sample right where they're grown. And here you're never far from the urban sophistication – and fine dining – of cities and towns such as Tours, Amboise, Blois and Saumur.

© MATT MUNRO / LONELY PLANET

ABOVE Start with strolls in Paris, then tour châteaux such as Saumur (left) in the Loire Valley.

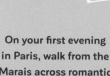
FOR THE LOVE OF GARDENS

⋙⟶ If you love flowers and plants, the château gardens of the Loire will engulf you in leafy bliss. At Chenonceau (www.chenonceau.com), you can stroll through a formal French garden established by Diane de Poitiers, mistress of King Henri II, as well as a rose garden laid out by her bitter rival Catherine de Médicis, his lawful wife. Chaumont-sur-Loire (www.domaine-chaumont.fr) is famed for its International Garden Festival and the 'living works of art' grown there each year. Perhaps the most romantic gardens are those surrounding Villandry (www.chateauvillandry.fr), whose Jardin d'Ornement uses intricate flower beds and geometrical hedges to portray four kinds of love: fickle, passionate, tender and tragic.

On your first evening in Paris, walk from the Marais across romantic Louis-Philippe Bridge to Île St-Louis, and then to Notre Dame Plaza. Return to Île de la Cité the next morning to see the inside of Cathédrale Notre Dame.

⋙⟶

Take the metro to Anvers and walk up to Montmartre, favourite hang-out of Belle Époque artists, for breathtaking views from the stairs in front of Sacré-Coeur Basilica.

⋙⟶

Hop on a train to Amboise (1¾ hours). By rental car, explore majestic châteaux such as Chambord, Blois, Chenonceau, Villandry, Langeais and Azay-le-Rideau, stopping by vineyards such as those around Château Moncontour (moncontour.com) to sample and buy wine.

© TTOURLET / 500PX

LEFT Chambord is the perfect place to start your love affair with the Loire's châteaux; in Paris (above), make like a local and grab picnic fare at a Latin Quarter market to eat by the Seine.

© MING TANG-EVANS / LONELY PLANET

© BRUNO DE HOGUES / GETTY IMAGES

Paris' Avenue des Champs-Élysées is not only grand, it's also impossibly romantic. Strolling 3.5km from the Louvre pyramid to the Arc de Triomphe takes you through flowery French-style gardens, including Jardin des Tuileries; across Place de la Concorde, with its magnificent colonnades and ancient Egyptian obelisk; and, on extra-wide sidewalks, past glorious 19th-century architecture.

To re-experience the serendipity and joy of discovering each other, head to the Loire Valley's magnificent Château de Chambord and climb the famous double-helix staircase – each of you on a different spiral, unseen by the other. Meet on the roof for a kiss!

DREAM DIGS

★ For the ultimate in Loire luxury, book a sumptuous room in the **Château de Brissac**, a towering, 204-room castle that's been the home of the Brissac family since 1502 – that's 18 generations! Lavishly decorated with period furnishings, the bedchambers will immerse you in the ambience and luxury of château life. (www.chateau-brissac.fr)

★ Near the Loire Valley town of Saumur, Irish expats Mary and Conor welcome you to the 18th-century **Château de Beaulieu** with a glass of *crémant de Saumur* (sparkling wine). To relax, you can sun yourself by the pool (next to the vineyard) or play billiards in the grand salon. (www. chateaudebeaulieu.fr)

THE HONEYMOON HANDBOOK

FLORENCE, TUSCANY & CINQUE TERRE, ITALY

○ Culture
○ Food & Drink
○ Outdoors

Artistic treasures, romantic hideaways and spectacular seascapes – this is the perfect marriage of culture, fine living and achingly beautiful scenery.

LEFT Tuscany's premier wine region Chianti, and its pretty villages, are just a short hop from the terracotta-roofed city of Florence (below).

Ever since the days of the 19th-century Grand Tour, travellers have been flocking to Florence in search of culture and romance. And it doesn't disappoint. Celebrated masterpieces flaunt their stuff at every turn, and museums such as the Galleria degli Uffizi and Museo del Bargello are awash with world-famous artworks. Its Renaissance streets are a spectacle in themselves and everywhere you go you're assailed by inspiring views. For that perfect sunset snapshot, head up to Piazzale Michelangelo and gaze down on the red-capped Duomo and the city's medieval skyline.

Extending south from Florence, the Chianti wine country is the ideal place to get away from it all and enjoy the simple pleasures of Tuscany – its quintessential landscapes, hearty regional food and fabulous local wine. Should the mood take you, there are one or two sights worth searching out, including the 11th-century Castello di Brolio and alfresco contemporary artworks at the Parco Sculture del Chianti.

To finish your trip on a high, head to the Cinque Terre for a blast of spectacular coastal scenery. The principle activities here are exploring the five picturesque villages, swimming, and walking the seafront Via dell'Amore. For a tougher challenge there's also serious hiking in the green, terraced hills that rise vertiginously above the sea.

THE HONEYMOON HANDBOOK

Itinerary

Start with a few days in Florence. Take in a museum or two, visit the Duomo, and hang out over an *aperitivo* on one of the city's theatrical piazzas.

≫⟶

Pick up a car and head south to Chianti. Enjoy the soothing scenery as you follow winding country roads to wineries, acclaimed farmhouse restaurants and charming rural retreats.

≫⟶

For the last leg, hop on a train and rattle over to the Cinque Terre. Here you can lap up the holiday vibe in the five quaint villages, splash around in the sea and hike in the green-capped hills.

DIAMOND TIP

SINCE HEAVY RAINS IN 2011, WALKING PATHS IN THE CINQUE TERRE HAVE BEEN SUBJECT TO PERIODIC CLOSURE. CHECK TRAIL INFORMATION AT WWW.PARCONAZIONALE5TERRE.IT BEFORE HEADING OUT.

© RILIND H / 500PX

© STEVANZZ / 500PX

LEFT Travelling north from La Spezia, colourful Riomaggiore, with its houses tumbling down to the sea, is the first of the Cinque Terre villages you'll encounter.

DREAM DIGS

★ For a taste of life as an aristocrat, the **Antica Torre di Via Tornabuoni 1** is a stylish boutique hotel in a graceful 14th-century *palazzo* near the Arno in Florence. Rooms are classically attired but what completely steals the show are the stunning views from the rooftop terrace – sip a breakfast cappuccino and swoon at Florence, laid out before you. (tornabuoni1.com)

★ The very epitome of rural chic, **Villa Sassolini** is an idyllic country hideaway. Set in dense forest 25km east of Radda in Chianti, it offers stylish, contemporary interiors, an intimate restaurant, and a lovely pool terrace. (www.villasassolini.it)

DAY-TRIPPING FROM CINQUE TERRE

⫸⟶ Northwest of the Cinque Terre, the Riviera di Levante makes for a great day trip with its perfectly coiffured towns and chic Italian seascapes. From the Cinque Terre, trains and seasonal boats run up to Santa Margherita, a charming town with handsome Liberty (art nouveau)-style buildings and an elegant seafront promenade. From there you can connect, by bus or boat, to Portofino – a picture-perfect village much beloved by holidaying celebs. Here you can browse designer shops and drink on the yacht-filled harbour or escape to the quiet trails of the Parco Natural Regionale di Portofino.

Of the many masterpieces on show in Florence, none is quite as dramatic as Michelangelo's *David*. This muscular 5.16m-high depiction of the Old Testament hero is one of the great icons of Western art and the sight of him at the Galleria dell'Accademia is nothing short of breathtaking.

—

One of the great joys of exploring the Chianti area is its wineries – some of which are centuries old. Many open their cellar doors to visitors, offering guided tours, tastings and sometimes even meals. A top spot is Antinori nel Chianti Classico (antinorichianticlassico.it; book ahead), which includes a rooftop restaurant at Bargino, 20km northwest of Greve.

THE HONEYMOON HANDBOOK

💎

DiAMOND TiP

FOR THE SAKE OF YOUR MARRIAGE, DON'T DRIVE INTO ANDALUCIA'S BiG CITY CENTRES, WHERE THE STREETS ARE NARROW AND OFTEN ONE WAY, AND PARKING IS A NIGHTMARE: SPEEDY TRAINS LINK SEVILLE, CÓRDOBA, MÁLAGA AND GRANADA.

Practicalities

✈ Seville, Málaga or Granada

LGBT-friendly ★★★★☆

🧳 Sunglasses, hats, sunscreen, light clothing and sensible shoes.

📅 May, June or September for sunny Andalucían weather minus the scorching heat of July to August.

$ $

○ Culture
○ Food & Drink
○ Relaxation

ANDALUCÍA, SPAIN

Simmering with southern-Spanish flavour, sun-soaked Andalucía bewitches with its Moorish monuments, vibrant cities, gleaming-white villages, fabulous food and sensationally scenic landscapes. It's undisputedly one of Spain's most romantic regions, delivering beauty and intrigue at every turn.

Few places fuel romance in the way multifaceted Andalucía does. This passionate southern pocket of Spain hosts a line-up of astonishingly beautiful World Heritage-listed monuments, many of which date back a thousand years to Moorish times. Seville's cathedral and Alcázar (fortress), Córdoba's Mezquita and Granada's Alhambra are the showstoppers, but there's plenty more for loved-up couples to discover. Throw in feisty flamenco, lively fiestas, patches of wide-open countryside and white towns teetering majestically atop sheer cliffs, and Andalucía makes an unforgettable honeymoon destination.

Sights aside, newly-weds can relish each other's company at steaming Arabic-style baths, disappear into the bustle of Granada's exotic *teterías* (teahouses) or simply soak up Spanish life by aimlessly wandering the cobbled lanes of Andalucía's atmospheric city *barrios* (neighbourhoods). Handsome historic hotels and character-packed guesthouses across the region ensure you'll always have a special oasis to retreat to.

This region is also

FROM TOP LEFT TO RIGHT Granada's hilltop Alhambra; Málaga; cafe culture in Granada's Albayzín district; Córdoba's Roman bridge.

© IVAN VDOVIN / GETTY IMAGES

© MATTES REN / GETTY IMAGES

Andalucía's 'Golden Triangle' comprises some of Spain's most fabled cities. Start with sizzling Seville; climb its cathedral's Islamic-origin Giralda tower, wander the splendid Alcázar and marvel at the Plaza de España's tile-work extravaganza.

≫⟶

Side-trip south from Seville to clifftop white town Arcos de la Frontera and its maze-like old town.

≫⟶

Take the train east to Córdoba, with its magical Mezquita, flower-festooned patios and historic allure.

≫⟶

Finish up with Granada's fantastic free tapas and Moorish architectural jewel, the Alhambra. For stunning sunset views head to the Mirador de San Nicolás: you'll be serenaded by flamenco buskers (but beware the bagsnatchers!).

home to a rich culinary scene. Enjoy lazing over lavishly long lunches before hunting down sublime sunset-gazing spots, or seek out tantalising tapas – the ultimate sharing bites (and famously free in Granada) – which you can feast on in tiny sizzling bars while savouring fine Spanish wines: just a typical night out in this part of the world.

RIGHT One of the greatest joys of travel in Andalucía is eating. Join locals at teeny tapas bars down cobbled alleyways – just be warned that most Spaniards wouldn't dream of dining before 9-10pm. Enjoy a siesta first...

© WILL HEAP / GETTY IMAGES

BEYOND THE GOLDEN TRIANGLE

≫⟶ With its myriad historical wonders, outdoors adventures and ridiculously romantic corners, Andalucía is a place newly-weds will love to linger. Time permitting, extend your trip beyond the Golden Triangle. Spend time in dynamic seaside Málaga exploring buzzy art galleries, sipping *tintos de verano* (red wine and lemonade) and hitting the sand in Picasso's hometown, then stroll above the spine-tingling Tajo gorge in spectacular Ronda. Outdoors-lovers could devote a few days to hiking or horse riding between whitewashed villages in Granada's majestic Sierra Nevada. Alternatively, seek out boutique-hotel bliss in the mysterious white town of Vejer de la Frontera and laze on the Costa de la Luz' breezy blonde beaches.

Towering above Granada's meandering alleyways, the Unesco-listed Alhambra (alhambra-tickets.es) is a mesmerising Moorish-origin world of tinkling fountains, glorious gardens, statue-studded patios and exquisite geometric design. Book ahead (especially in June to August) and explore it during early-morning or late-evening slots, or on atmospheric after-dark visits.

From expertly choreographed *tablaos* to raw, impromptu *peñas* (clubs), nothing ignites passion like foot-stomping flamenco music and dance. Catch authentic flamenco at Seville's Casa de la Memoria (casadelamemoria.es) or Granada's Peña La Platería (laplateria.org.es), apparently Spain's oldest aficionados' club.

DREAM DIGS

★ **Casa 1800** is a sumptuous, centrally positioned beauty in Seville, blending palatial 19th-century charm with coolly contemporary comforts, superb service, a sleek rooftop pool and a deck gazing out on the Giralda. The complimentary *merienda* (afternoon tea) is a delight. For an ultra-special treat, splash out on a luxurious jacuzzi-equipped terrace suite. (www.hotelcasa1800sevilla.com)

★ Fancy snoozing in a slickly converted 19th-century palace? **Hotel Hospes Palacio de los Patos** in Granada is bold, minimalist boutique-chic, with majestic period features, brilliant breakfasts and flowers laid out on your bed. Canoodle in the dreamy Andalucian garden and on-site spa. (www.hospes.com)

THE HONEYMOON HANDBOOK

© LOTTIE DAVIES / LONELY PLANET

© MATTHEW WILLIAMS-ELLIS / GETTY IMAGES

© CORY SCHADT / 500PX

DIAMOND TIP

GETTING AROUND CROATIA'S COASTAL DESTINATIONS BY SEAPLANE IS A SCENIC TIME-SAVER. EUROPEAN COASTAL AIRLINES OFFERS FLIGHTS BETWEEN MAJOR MAINLAND AND ISLAND DESTINATIONS. (WWW.EC-AIR.EU)

Practicalities

✈ Dubrovnik

LGBT-friendly ★★★★☆

💼 Pack light but smart – bring flip-flops and water shoes (sea urchins abound), sunblock, sunhat and mosquito repellant.

📅 The best time to go is June and September; July and August are peak periods, meaning high crowds and high costs.

$ / $

ABOVE Look familiar? Dubrovnik starred as Westeros in *Game of Thrones*; you can visit the Pakleni Islands (left) from Hvar.

CROATiA

Few places in the world hold as much charm as Croatia's island-speckled coast. With more than 1000 isles strung between sapphire seas, its archipelagos of secluded coves and small historic outposts are perfect for disappearing with your loved one.

○ Relaxation
○ Beach
○ Outdoors

151   THE HONEYMOON HANDBOOK

© PHOTOGRAPHER / IMAGE LIBRARY

Itinerary

⫸⟶ Get lost in Split's harbourside Diocletian's Palace before partaking in its buzzy local nightlife.

⫸⟶ Take a catamaran to sun-splashed Hvar and clamber up to the hilltop fortress for eye-popping views of the town, the harbour and Pakleni Islands.

⫸⟶ Move on to Korčula island, stock up on traditional island sweets at Cukarin bakery in its namesake town and amble through the history-rich streets.

⫸⟶ End your trip in Dubrovnik. Walk its city walls at sunset and have a romantic drink at a cliffside bar, before escaping town for a swim off the lush isle of Lokrum or a visit to the Elafiti archipelago.

ABOVE Classy Hvar has cobbled-street charm but also an air of sophistication in its restaurants and bars.

The Adriatic coast of Croatia is ideal for cosying up with your darling, with an isle to suit every couple's style. Think mild Mediterranean climate, deliciously fresh seafood, history-packed seaside towns, pine-backed pebble beaches and gorgeously clean sea.

Even the more popular islands have nooks and crannies you can escape to. Take well-loved (and much-visited) Hvar, for instance, with its namesake town featuring swanky beach bars and ancient Venetian townhouses rising up the hillsides – a short boat ride from here whisks you to the Pakleni Islands, a pretty, deserted string of pine-shaded speckles.

The Dalmatian mainland city of Split invites for an aimless amble around the maze of passages and courtyards of its Diocletian's Palace, a Roman quarter where the ancient walls throb with life and history. The remote island of Vis is the coast's best-kept secret, a former military outpost once closed off to the public and now the connoisseur's choice for top food and beaches, multihued swimming caves and a boho vibe. Korčula island, where Marco Polo is said to have been born, showcases Venetian architecture and fairytale streetscapes.

And then there's the crown jewel of Dalmatia's coast, Dubrovnik, with its fabled old town of terracotta roofs, marbled lanes and age-old towers, all surrounded by the cerulean sea.

DREAM DIGS

★ The perfect castaway escape for couples, **Radej Retreat for Conscious Living** nestles on an uninhabited islet near Murter. Run by a Croatian-French pair, this hideaway has one sweet stone cottage for two, steps from the sea. The stay includes vegetarian meals made with local ingredients, heavenly massages and alfresco yoga. (radej-retreat.hr)

★ **Palagruža**, on Croatia's most remote isle, offers a frontier experience at its 1875 lighthouse perched atop a 90m-high rock, and an array of endemic species of flora and fauna. According to local lore, Pope Alexander III visited in 1177 and fell head over heels with the outpost. (www.lighthouses-croatia.com)

HORSEBACK RIDING & WINE TASTING

⟫⟶ Bond with your partner on horseback in Dubrovnik's hinterland, on a slow ride through the wild Konavle region with its olive groves and pine forests toward the rocky seaside. This jaunt features a romantic snack break with sweeping coastal views. To tickle your senses more extravagantly, book a six-course meal at the spectacular Saints Hills Winery on Pelješac peninsula. The inventive menus showcase dishes such as fresh oysters with sweet chilli sauce made with peppers from the nearby Neretva valley, and black risotto chips with cuttlefish salad. Get into the mood with the vineyard's full-bodied Dingač red. Both experiences can be booked via Journey2Croatia (www.journey2croatia.com).

With its 1246 islands dotting the Adriatic coast, Croatia is made for sailing. Charter a boat with a company such as Sails of Croatia (sailsofcroatia.com) for the duration of your trip or take a short sailing jaunt. The isle of Vis is a favourite for couples with its clutch of restaurants and beaches, plus heavenly swimming caves a boat ride away.

—

Explore Hvar's offbeat side with an offroad adventure with Secret Hvar (secrethvar.com). You'll see abandoned ancient villages and fragrant fields of lavender before stopping at a top-rate winery for a tasting of plavac, the local red. Then take a sunset sail around the bays and coves of the Pakleni Islands.

DIAMOND TIP

AURORAL ACTIVITY IS MEASURED IN KP (KP0 LOW, KP9 HIGH); MOST GEOMAGNETIC STORMS ARE NOT THAT STRONG – KP1–KP3 – AND ARE ONLY VISIBLE BETWEEN 66°N AND 69°N. HEAD TO THIS LATITUDE FOR YOUR BEST CHANCE OF A SIGHTING.

LAPLAND, FINLAND

Nothing will put a sparkle in your honeymoon quite like the northern lights. Even better, in snow-cloaked Finnish Lapland you have the chance to see this supernatural spectacle while cuddled up together in bed, before getting out in the snow.

Some say the northern lights are a lucky omen – that a child conceived beneath its ethereal glow will be prosperous and blessed. Science may not back this up, but witnessing the magical ballet of the aurora borealis is undeniably romantic. Especially if you don't have to freeze your extremities off while you watch.

Deep in Finnish Lapland, cold-averse couples have the chance to canoodle under the revontulet (meaning 'fox fires' – the Finnish phrase for the aurora) in comfort. Glass-roofed igloos with double beds and fluffy throws provide private cocoons of cosiness from which to keep an all-night vigil – though lodges also offer

'aurora alert' bleepers that will wake you if the lights come out to play. Even if they don't, the stars visible in these light-pollution-free wildernesses are impressive enough on their own.

Of course, there's no point coming all the way to the Arctic Circle just to lie in bed, even on honeymoon. In wintertime, Lapland's snow-smothered lakes, hills and forests turn into a sparkly playground. Cuddle up under reindeer skins on bell-jingly sleigh rides; tie on snowshoes or cross-country skis for a cheek-rosying escapade; or hop onto a snowmobile to zip across the frozen tundra together. Then warm up in a traditional Finnish sauna – clothing optional.

© MASSIMOFUSARO / GETTY IMAGES

LEFT & ABOVE Night rainbows of aurora activity and daytime husky-sledding adventures are hallmarks of travel in Lapland.

BELOW Come winter or summer, the Finnish love nothing better than time in a sauna cabin.

FEELING MUSHY ON A HUSKY SAFARI

⫸⟶ Dashing through the icy wilds behind a pack of eager hounds, no sounds breaking the silence except the slicing of snow and the odd enthusiastic howl – this is the ultimate way to experience the Arctic. While it's possible, and fun, to arrange short husky-sled excursions, to really bond with your loved one consider a multi-day expedition. An expert will teach you how to look after and mush (drive) your own teams of four to six dogs, and guide you across frozen lakes and pristine, snow-cloaked forests. Nights are spent sleeping out in remote stove-warmed cabins, far away from the rest of the world. (www.artisantravel.co.uk/holidays/husky-safari-holiday)

© RYHOR BRUYEU / IGETTY IMAGES

Get acclimatised to the cold right away, exploring the wilds by snowmobile, husky sled or snowshoes.

⫸⟶

Spend nights searching for the northern lights, perhaps by snowmobile or on skis. Splash out on a private sledge safari, to aurora-watch all alone.

⫸⟶

Spend at least one night in a private, glass-roofed igloo, where you can drink chilled fizz in a warm bubble and gaze up at the stars.

⫸⟶

You could end the trip with a lazier day, perhaps visiting a museum about the indigenous Sami people, working up a sweat in the sauna, tucking into reindeer stew, then curling up by an open fire.

ABOVE Glass-domed igloos provide unparallelled aurora-viewing opportunities at the Kakslauttanen resort deep in Lapland.

© KAKSLAUTTANEN

© KAKSLAUTTANEN

Take turns riding pillion on a two-person snowmobile, heading out into the frozen forests after dark to search for the northern lights on an aurora safari. Pull over in a spot with open views of the skies, share a thermos of hot lingonberry juice and keep your fingers crossed for aurora action.

—

Sweat together in a private, stove-heated sauna – a Finnish tradition. Pour water onto the hot stones for extra steaminess then, when you can sweat no more, dash outside to roll in the snow (or take a cold shower). Smack each other with a *vihta* (birch-branch bundle) for increased circulatory stimulation.

DREAM DIGS

★ At **Kakslauttanen** you can book an igloo with a dome of special thermal glass, which keeps the heat in without frosting up, giving you clear views of the aurora-smeared sky while remaining toasty warm. Kakslauttanen's Kelo-Glass Igloos combine the glass domes with cosy log cabins, which have fireplaces and private saunas too. (kakslauttanen.fi)

★ The Aurora Bubbles at **Nellim Wilderness Hotel** are private pods set a short, snowy stroll from Nellim's main lodge, with gloriously warm, pine-planked bedrooms and huge, north-facing, frost-free dome windows. You can stare up at the stars and any dancing lights from under your duvet. (www.nellim.fi)

NOTES

NOTES

NOTES

NOTES

NOTES

NOTES

NOTES

NOTES

ABOUT THE AUTHORS

Sarah Baxter
Travel writer and author Sarah hasn't been on a honeymoon herself, but loves planning other people's: she was editor of Unique Honeymoons magazine, and strives to seek out offbeat romantic spots.

Greg Benchwick
Greg first travelled to Nicaragua in 1995. Since then, Greg's written dozens of Lonely Planet books, interviewed heads-of-state and Grammy-award winners, and sought romance in some of the planet's most remote corners.

Sara Benson
Sara is a travel and outdoor adventure writer who spent her own honeymoon hopping between Hawaiian Islands, from volcanic peaks to soft, sandy beaches.

Heather Carswell
Heather is a London-based writer and PR. Her travels have taken her across the globe, but her heart remains in Southeast Asia.

Duncan Garwood
Since moving to Italy and getting married in Taranto, Duncan has travelled extensively in his adopted homeland and worked on a raft of Lonely Planet Italy titles.

John Hecht
Mexico-based John has authored more than a dozen Lonely Planet books, including two editions of Cancún, Cozumel & the Yucatán.

Carolyn B. Heller
Vancouver-based travel writer Carolyn honeymooned by the ocean but loves the mountains, too. A contributor to more than 50 travel guides, she's explored 40+ countries on six continents.

adam karlin
Adam has worked on over 50 Lonely Planet guidebooks, including Florida, Botswana, Kenya and India. He spent his honeymoon in Nashville, and it was pretty amazing.

Olivia Knight
Olivia is the founder of honeymoon fund patchworkit.com. She travels regularly with her husband and two children and writes about honeymoons for Wedding Ideas and You and Your Wedding.

Anja Mutic
Travel writer Anja splits time between New York and Croatia. She has written for publications including National Geographic Traveler, The Wall Street Journal and BBC Travel. everthenomad.com.

Isabella Noble
Isabella is a Spain specialist travel journalist for Lonely Planet and Telegraph Travel, in love with Andalucía, where she grew up. She also covers India, Southeast Asia, Britain and beyond.

Etain O'Carroll
Travel writer Etain has authored over 30 Lonely Planet books as well as writing for magazines and newspapers while indulging a love of travel off the beaten track.

Lorna Parkes
A former Lonely Planet destination editor for the Caribbean, Central America and Iberia in Europe, in a past life Lorna also used to edit Bride Destination magazine in Australia. Honeymoon planning is one of her callings.

Matt Phillips
With 15 years of extensive travel across Africa – some of it luxurious,

CHAPTER 78

At eight o'clock he walked through the main entrance to the Swedish Navy Headquarters on Skeppsholmen. An adjutant invited him to sit down and wait as not everybody on the committee had arrived. A vice admiral who lived out at Djursholm had telegraphed to say that he would be late.

Tobiasson-Svartman shuddered in the cold corridor. He listened to some bugle calls drifting in through the window, followed by the dull thud of a single artillery shot.

After half an hour or so the adjutant informed him that the committee was ready to receive him. He entered a room with previous Admirals of the Fleet staring down at him from the walls. The committee comprised two vice admirals, a captain and a lieutenant whose job it was to keep the minutes. A chair had been placed in readiness for him, in front of the committee who were sitting in a row behind a table covered in a green baize.

Vice Admiral Lars H:son-Lydenfeldt was the chairman. For many years he had been the driving force behind efforts to increase the Swedish Navy's operating capabilities. He had a reputation of being impatient and arrogant, and dominated all those around him by means of sudden outbursts of fury. He invited Tobiasson-Svartman to sit down.

'Your work is impressive,' he said. 'You seem to have that rare thing, a passion for secret military navigable channels. Is that true?'

'I just try to do my job to the best of my ability.'

The vice admiral shook his head impatiently.

'Every single member of the Swedish Navy does his job to the best of his ability. Or at least one can assume that there are not too many idlers and layabouts. I'm talking about something different. Passion. Do you understand?'

'I understand.'

'Then perhaps you would be kind enough to answer my question?'

Tobiasson-Svartman thought about his dream of finding a depth too deep to measure.

'It is exciting to record things that cannot immediately be taken in and comprehended.'

The vice admiral looked doubtfully at him, but decided to accept the answer.

'What you say is understandable. I thought something similar myself in my younger days. But what you thought in your youth, you forget in your manhood and only recall it in your old age.'

The vice admiral sat up straight and held up a chart.

'Our commander-in-chief will receive the chart with the new stretches of channel at Sandsänkan in the new year. A couple of our frigates will test them out during night manoeuvres in differing weather conditions.'

He reached for another chart.

'Gamlebyviken,' he said. 'The approach to the narrow bay. Cramped, existing depth soundings doubtful, constant silting up that hasn't been checked since the 1840s. Well, Commander Svartman, have you been informed that we are counting on you to undertake this mission in the new year?'

'Yes, I have been informed.'

'In our judgement this mission is important and will be given priority. Other measuring operations will be postponed for the time being, since the war means that vessels are needed for other duties.'

'I am ready to start at once.'

'Excellent. You will receive your instructions immediately after Christmas.'

The vice admiral glanced at the lieutenant who was keeping the minutes.

'On 27 December, 08.45 hours,' the lieutenant said.

The vice admiral nodded.

'So, that's that. Has any member of the committee any questions?'

Captain Hansson, who was the oldest person present, with experience